Team Roles at Work

Meredith Belbin

Pfeiffer
& COMPANY

Amsterdam • Johannesburg • Oxford
San Diego • Sydney • Toronto

© Butterworth-Heinemann Ltd, 1981
ISBN 0 7506 0925 7

Originally published by
Butterworth-Heinemann Ltd
Linacre House, Jordan Hill, Oxford OX2 8DP

A MEMBER OF THE REED ELSEVIER GROUP

Published in the U.S. by
Pfeiffer & Company
8517 Production Avenue
San Diego, CA 92121-2280
(619) 578-5900, FAX (619) 578-2042

ISBN 0-88390-441-1

Printed in the United States of America

This book is printed on acid-free, recycled stock that meets or exceeds the
minimum GPO and EPA specifications for recycled paper.

Contents

Preface

It was a matter of surprise for myself and my publishers that my earlier book *Management Teams: Why They Succeed Or Fail* should have reached its peak in sales nine years after being first published. The explanation, apparently, was that a new way of describing roles and relationships at work had gradually percolated into the wider language of industry and so created its own momentum. This movement was given its main push by two broad groups of people. The first comprised those who work in management education, including industrial trainers. The second group was made up of active practitioners, especially those charged with the urgent need of improving results from small project teams or new business ventures.

The spread of team-role theory and ideas is therefore partly due to the influence and initiatives of many whom I have never met. Of those I have, several have struck me as well placed to write a sequel to the book themselves on the basis of their insightful application of current theory and the wealth of their experiences.

Nevertheless, some responsibilities inevitably fall my way. For some time I have felt the need to write a follow-up book as a result of the many questions asked at lectures and the letters I have received from many different parts of the globe. Pressures began to mount in the mind whenever I reflected that the answers I gave at the time were not as adequate as I would have wished. Wisdom is always assisted in due course by the beneficence of time and hindsight.

The second factor that has persuaded me to put finger to keyboard is that during the last ten years computerization of data has rendered many difficult issues much easier to understand. Our perspective changed as more variables could be considered and their interactions assessed. The inclusion of observer material, along with the further discovery that the specific demands of given jobs had team-role implications, added value to the original team-role concepts. In essence, the range of inputs could be extended, filtered, normalized and computer processed into team-role language to produce a wide range of personnel related outputs in a few seconds. Thereafter, the problem became one of how best to manage this new range of information and advice. Here much experience has been gained on which to report.

For the benefit of prospective readers, a few words may be said about the nature of the material covered in the chapters that lie ahead. The first port of call relates to the way in which work has been assigned throughout the ages. From the earliest times roles were cast from stereotypes about particular groupings of people. Later, a developing recognition of individual aptitudes and skills brought about a revolution in the way in which work was organized. That individuality was preserved through formal job titles arranged in strict hierarchies. But in due course the disadvantages of sharply differentiating job territories in well-ordered organizations threatened to outweigh the advantages. Responsibilities became fragmented, communication barriers grew and the bureaucracy that resulted made it difficult to tackle large issues in a holistic fashion. As these faults became increasingly apparent, a new form of awareness set in. It was gradually recognized that the vitality of groups depends on interdependence and co-operation between members. Team-role language grew in response to this demand and its nature, mechanism and implications are explained.

The middle section of the book deals with the operational strategies now available to executives. Team-role theory and data have a special part to play in self-management, in the management of others and in the resolution of conflict. Here there are ideas and techniques that can be learned to advantage.

The concluding chapters address the more political aspects of team-role management. The move from solo leadership to team leadership, problems of succession in management and the future shape of organization are examined in the light of newly acquired understanding and experience.

The author, in writing this book, is deeply indebted to the many who have contributed in work and ideas from the earliest days of experimentation at Henley, through the development of the information technology that has allowed us to enter so many uncharted waters, to more recent days when pioneers have valiantly introduced team-role concepts and practices in many countries overseas. While I hesitate to mention names for fear of leaving out of account those who merit mention, I cannot let the occasion pass without saying a few words about those who have rendered special help since the earlier book was written.

First, there are those who have read the draft and made helpful suggestions, comprising my son and colleague, Nigel Belbin; Dr Jeanne

Fisher, who has been there to compensate for my weaknesses from the earliest days to the very last moment; Dr Andrew Life, an esteemed colleague from the Henley days and now retired; Dr Dawie Gouws in South Africa and now New Zealand, a source of much wisdom; Dr David Marriott and John Burns, both valued colleagues over many years in Australia; and finally Kathryn Grant from Butterworth-Heinemann who has also rendered encouragement throughout. Secondly, there are those who have contributed in other ways. They include Tony Glaze, former Manpower Development Director of Cadbury Schweppes and now Managing Director of Group Personnel, a close colleague on some major management reconstructions; Jeff Hayden who has carried out experiments with teams on a worldwide scale; Charles Dodd of Cambridgeshire County Council who has been there from start to finish with advice and encouragement; Mike Woods who has written about the application of the ideas so well; Rob Groen of Holland, my most long-standing colleague who I see less frequently than I would wish; Tom Noonan and Dr Len Goodstein who have combined so effectively to open up interest in the United States, and many others whom I have met more fleetingly yet who have impressed me with the talent they have demonstrated on particular projects.

Creative skills are embodied as much in the application of work as in its origination and I hope that this book will stimulate new ways of applying team-role theory. The pages that follow may be read passively for interest and enlightenment (if that is what they deserve). Or they can prompt some new action depending on what is relevant to the reader's circumstances. It is, of course, my wish that most readers will prefer the latter option.

Meredith Belbin

1 *A short history of roles at work*

This book is about the establishment of roles within a team where the assumption of duties and responsibilities depends on a measure of self-discovery combined with a perception of the needs of the team as a whole.

If it is argued that roles are not normally brought about in that way, I would have to agree. Usually, people are given roles; they do not find them. Nor for that matter do they associate work with teams. Yet I would claim that advanced teamwork is one of the most efficient ways we know of accomplishing complex tasks and missions.

The concept of the team itself, as it relates to work, is of comparatively recent origin. That is so for two reasons: first, because teams, where the players play a different part but enjoy broadly equal status, have no precedents in the broad political history of mankind, with perhaps one exception that I will deal with shortly; and second because the assignment of duties and responsibilities has been governed by traditional rules and conventions so deeply embedded that they still operate as the primary determinants of roles in the world around us. So it is important to heed the nature of these forces if we are to proceed, for, in the complex societies of our times, nothing ever begins on a blank sheet.

If the word 'teams' does not appear in recorded history, it is hardly surprising, since it would hardly be a fitting description of the many key groupings of people that have significantly affected events over the last three thousand years. Yet in an earlier age, when closely knit bands of nomadic hunters and gatherers roamed the earth, social life was very different from what followed later. Evidence from surviving indigenous peoples suggests a pattern of social behaviour marked by its elemental, spontaneous and sharing character. These small dynamic groups, closely related in kin, commonly matrilineal in descent, and matrilocal in their places of residence, developed relationships that owed little to the exercise of personal power. The primaeval team in which women played so important a part belonged to an age that eventually gave way to, or was overwhelmed by, patriarchal society.

The nature of working relationships changed with the building of towns and cities along with the settlement and ownership of large tracts of territory. For as the gains in material culture became worth defending, evolution exerted its unrelenting laws. The survival of the fittest meant that ascendancy was conferred on the possessors of superior weapons. And, inevitably, those possessors discovered that what could be used in defence was of equal value in attack; that weapons constituted investments, offering conspicuous rewards in the harvests of war — booty, tribute, growing empires and a vanquished people who could provide wives, concubines or slaves or, failing that, might be exterminated at will. (The Mongol and Ottoman empires, the largest the world had ever seen, owed their remarkable rate of expansion from so small a base to the discovery of a winning formula: interbreeding with the available women in the conquered lands and killing all but the most submissive men. So their empires grew as their kinship expanded.)

As primaeval teams recede, tyrannical order develops

But weapons and violence alone were not enough to give this new order of society permanence. Something extra was needed. That something was disciplined organiz1tion and it was conferred by patriarchy based on the authority of the war leader. Its uniform theme was the exertion of, and respect for, power.

Just as power regulated dealings between states, turning some nations into imperial masters and others into the subjugated, power was directed inwardly as much as outwardly. It was the key to organization within the state — in political or social spheres no less than in the military. Power was wielded by the implied threat of force, or overtly by terror, commonly aided by resort to torture and even, in some societies, by human sacrifice.

Power, by its nature, starts at the top and is exercised downwards through a succession of subordinate relationships. Its mode of operation ensured that the key issues of politics hinged on the whims and personality of the ruler. And, as the ruler aged, all attention turned to succession. Where would-be heirs could point to no acknowledged rules to bolster their claims, succession became literally a subject of life and death. Monarchs were fortunate if they died peacefully in their beds. Sons murdered fathers in their haste to seize the throne. Rulers surrounded themselves with ever-watchful bodyguards and the duties of administration were passed to eunuchs, whose ambitions to install their own line were limited by the destruction of their capacity to reproduce. But even so, plots for assassination could still be hatched from afar. Poisoning became the favoured long-range weapon; food tasting a common security occupation.

Those who ruled their empires by the sword may have been preoccupied with their own well-being and personal ambitions. But tyranny had one positive outcome. It showed what a disciplined organization, even in its harshest forms, can accomplish.

The level of economic and cultural success that each empire reached now depended on a new governing factor — the division of labour. The higher the level of achievement, the more intricate this division became. The assigning of duties and tasks necessary to maintain the system demands complex handling; for every successful system that uses labour, whether imperial or industrial, has to settle the recurring question — according to what principles should work be distributed?

Several types of solution were available. Whatever formula was chosen had an enormous bearing on the vitality of the system and on the survival value of the society that adopted it.

Some traditional ways of assigning people to work roles

It is not in the nature of autocratic rulers to consult servants and underlings or to weigh up their preferences when distributing duties and responsibilities. A few favourites may have enjoyed the pick of appointments. But the great mass of people had no say in the matter. Their work was determined according to their station.

The notions of rulers about what work particular people should and should not be doing may be based on prejudice and often on falsehoods. But whatever their merits or otherwise, such beliefs ensure that the required work gets done. By classifying people, work schedules are more easily arranged. So to understand the productive forces of society and its dynamic mechanisms, one should first look at how work is assigned to those who are to undertake it.

When scheduled work began — of the type needed to develop major well-planned undertakings — only a limited range of possibilities existed. The most straightforward rules for allotting differentiated duties involved a visual classification of people by age, gender and race.

That classification has such universality of application that it is no surprise it is alive and well today. In many contemporary societies it remains, as it has done for countless ages, the principal determinant of the rank and occupational positions in which people find themselves.

The most senior person gets the job

One of the most favoured differentiators of status is seniority. Individuals line up for jobs, responsibility and promotion in a sequential order where the first to arrive in service and employment has the highest claim. All the jobs are similarly ranked on the ladder of a hierarchy. As the years pass by, the candidates move up a rung and occupy positions with the higher status.

The premium placed on seniority was much in evidence at the turn of the last century. A typical example was set by the railways. A newcomer would be given a station or track job before being allowed on to a locomotive. The entry job would then be as fireman. That title denoted a stoker busily shovelling coals into the boiler. Many years would pass before he was allowed to act as a locomotive driver. That was the route forward. There was no other.

An everyday example can be witnessed in a restaurant. There, an under-waiter is ranked below a waiter, who in turn is less important than a wine waiter, above whom stands the head waiter. Each job involves different tasks, performance in which scarcely prepares the job holder for the position above. But one unwritten code applies — no under-waiter would ever be appointed who was older than a head waiter.

A seeming justification of the seniority principle is that age and experience convey confidence and wisdom (as once must have been true before the age of literacy). The principle is therefore traditional, with the conservative nature of its code ensuring the unwavering support of the establishment. As has been the case in China for centuries, status is attached to looking old. The practical advantage of the age and seniority principle is that anyone can check that no-one has been promoted out of turn. At the same time, those who have any reason to be disappointed can console themselves with the thought that their turn will eventually come.

Here it is remarkable how a long-standing principle has lately been turned on its head. In the sunrise industries, age and experience have given way to an emphasis on youth, vigour and recency of education. For those who fail to match these requirements, the prospects are poor. As the passage of years renders them 'past it', the disappointed are consigned to the legendary 'scrap-heap'. So age still serves, even in its perverse form, as a visual marker for assigning work.

The impact of gender

There is another simple principle, of ancient origins, which from time immemorial has governed the allocation of tasks and responsibilities. That principle is gender.

Men and women in most societies and firms characteristically do different jobs. The distinction in domains is so basic that in most languages − with the notable exception of English − nouns are either feminine or masculine. (That in some languages the compromise of neuter has introduced a grey zone does no more than mask the fundamental division.) The fact that there is no uniformity in what constitutes the orbits of masculinity and femininity matters less than the fact that the division exists at all. For by existing it simplifies decision-making in terms of the roles people play. A dynamic market entrepreneur in West Africa is likely to be female, in India and China male. It is not aptitude but how the gender factor is treated in culture that largely determines the differences in job opportunities.

Those biophysical twins, age and gender, are at their most powerful in their bearing on work roles when they operate in combination. There we encounter a powerful consolidating factor − initiation ceremonies or 'rites of passage'. These are kept rigorously separate for men and women as they move up the age scale. In tribal society these often gain an added emphasis through secret ceremonies. Emphasis is added through physical mutilation, e.g. male adolescent circumcision and its female equivalent, clitoridectomy, and by wearing distinguishing clothing or other forms of decoration. These transition points may strike one as primitive and often brutal. But they have a function. For they serve as frontiers, introducing, as they are passed through, new and socially accepted forms of work and privilege.

Age and gender have offered a means of separating roles, so bringing together complementary work activities throughout the history of mankind. But in due course, as the population filled the land, and intertribal and imperial conflicts became more intense, skirmishes gave way to conquests. There were the victors and there were the vanquished. And now a new principle became available for assigning roles at work, for those features of appearance that had hitherto marked out enemies now offered a special opportunity for constructive exploitation. The new formula for assigning work took in racial segregation and stratification. And so it came about that peoples of different stock took on different working roles.

Racial roles and hierarchies

Virtually all the early cities about which we have historical evidence were built up on ghettos. Cities were assemblies of peoples chosen for their specialist tribal skills. Inevitably, they looked physically different from one another. The ethnic factor played a major part in channelling them into distinctive occupations. Trades were passed from father to son and shared to some extent within their own community, but were nearly always hidden from outsiders.

Manpower policies thus have an ancient lineage, accounting for much of the belief that different peoples have different talents for particular classes of work. So strong was this belief that whenever one empire overran another in the ancient world, it was customary for the new ruler to transplant that source of wealth creation, the ghetto of skilled tradesmen, from the old city to the new capital.

So it was when Cairo fell to the Ottoman empire. Then, Selim the Grim uprooted the peoples of the most useful ghettos and resited them in Byzantium. As a consequence, Cairo never regained its former pre-eminence in the ancient world.

Because people in ghettos looked different, one could recognize or even assume their occupation. In due course, as empires expanded, these ethnic variations signified not merely the rich trade tapestries of cities but also different positions in the hierarchy of empire. This gradation was extended by bringing in and finding a place for slaves. Because conquered peoples belonged to different tribes and races, who were overcome in different circumstances, their positions within the system varied. The best positions would go to those who by their classification enjoyed superior status. For example, a Greek slave would typically end up as a tutor in a Roman patrician family. The losers became the hewers of wood and the drawers of water, or, in Roman times, the harshly treated labourers who toiled on the latifundia. Slaves who distinguished themselves through their work performance became emancipated and so moved one step up the social and work ladder. Yet race, and its junior cousin, tribe, still remained primary factors in marking out positions within the complexity of empire.

To this day, in liberally minded cities, different ethnic groups are still attached to certain trades, industries and professions. A balance between these ethnic groups can therefore enrich the life of the city. Moreover, much is to be gained for the groups themselves. There are social and cultural advantages both in passing on special skills within family groups and in restricting knowledge.

Yet the corollary is that those who start in disadvantaged positions face an uphill climb in rising to higher things whatever their talents. Progress is hardly possible for those outside the favoured circle until the old stereotypes are broken down.

The rise of the free city

These age-old conventional systems for assigning people to work had their part to play in expanding the productive base of society. But their greatest limitation to continued development was that they neglected individual differences. There was no place for those glittering and unexpected talents that often rear their heads in the most unexpected places. Personal behaviour was circumscribed by those stereotypes that attach to membership of an identified group. Individuality could find no place in such societies – a condition still to be witnessed in large parts of the world today. The acceptance of individual differences in the population at large did not enter the social and political scene until the power structures of empires and associated tyrannies began to crumble.

The opportunities first arose when small city states laid down their roots beyond the reach of powerful empires. So it was that Miletus, famed for such great thinkers as Heraclitus and Hippocrates, achieved its trading and cultural pre-eminence on the rocky coasts of Asia Minor; similarly Knossos on the apparently undefended island of Crete, Rhodes and Samos in the Aegean, Athens in the age of Pericles, or Corinth on the isthmus of the Peloponnese and its later colony, Syracuse, on Sicily. So it was that Venice established itself on sand dunes in the North Adriatic out of reach of invading Goths and Vandals; or Aigues Mortes, that remarkable and well-preserved walled city, set in a salt marsh on the Camargue and beyond the easy grasp of the Bourbons; or the cities of Armenia and Georgia in the mountain

Era	Criteria for assigning work	Method
Pre-industrial	By category: • Age • Sex • Tribe • Class	Visual inspection
Industrial	By qualifications: • Trade skills • Experience • Education	Certificates Selection panel
Post-industrial	By person shape: • Team role • Personal orientation	Computer matching Counselling interview

Figure 1.1 *Human resource strategies throughout the ages*

fastnesses of the Caucasus, protected from the ravages of the Mongol and Ottoman empires; or the independent Swiss cantons, founded by Huguenot artisans, protected in their remote mountain strongholds from the oppressive forces of the French monarchy; or the Baltic cities of the Hanseatic League spreading skills and enlightenment well beyond the Baltic itself; or the city states of Florence, Siena, Bologna, Assisi and others on the Italian peninsula, flourishing during the Renaissance before mega empires could once again resume their onward march.

These cities that had so much in common, over an extensive time span, owed their prosperity to their skills in craftmanship, small-scale industry and trading. They were small enough to make their own rules and to defy the conventions governing permitted work behaviour in larger-scale societies. They became beacons of opportunity. That was the state of affairs that prevailed with Athens in its heyday; for it welcomed skilled artisans, encouraged them to settle, allowed them to take out citizenship and in consequence became a magnet for the most talented in the Greek-speaking world. Such was the manpower policy that underlay its prosperity and cultural achievement.

The fluidity in movement that a trading community permits and

encourages, along with a recognition of the gains which the production of saleable goods offers, changed the way in which work was
regarded. A new valuation was placed on human skills and human
perfectibility, an emphasis often seen in the characteristic art forms
of these cultures.

Skilled labour in a free market

Under such conditions the scene was now set for the appearance of a
new operating principle in the assignment of work. Instead of relying
on the mechanistic classification of people for work according to
gender, age and race, another consideration came to the fore. That
consideration was individual skill.

In a free city, the road to success lay in acquiring a trade or
entering a profession. Any teacher of a trade or profession was in
demand. The ambitious sought an apprenticeship. Such was the
demand that it was common practice for apprentices to pay, rather
than to be paid by, the masters they served.

A journeyman (i.e. qualified craftsman) needed to establish his
credentials to the world at large. The age-old badges of work identity —
age, gender or race — could no longer offer the requisite cues. So how
was it to be done?

The answer had to be a written document authenticated by the master
under whom the apprentice had served. That in turn quickened the
quest for a general education; for documents are of little use unless
they can be read.

The path that had been opened up by city states over a long period
was widened by the industrial revolution until it became general
practice.

A person's work-role in life was no longer set by age, gender or race
but was conditioned by education and training, factors in limited
supply and therefore cherished all the more on that account. A job
title became a means of self-description. People would identify themselves in terms of what they had learned and what they were qualified
to do. So they were carpenters, turners and smiths — words which
became common surnames — or they collected at the highest status
level some professional title to announce both their occupation and
their identity. Self-projection of this nature was possible and even
desirable. People were free to move in a free labour market and to
take up any job offered, so it was in their interests that others should

know who they were in an occupational sense. Workers joined trade unions just as craftsmen had joined guilds.

A dilemma in work identity

The growth in personal liberty that small city states first offered, and which the industrial revolution enlarged, produced a new type of division of labour. It was one that gave scope to individual skills and talents. It meant that the contribution which each worker offered was no longer restricted by the straitjacket of social stereotyping. New talents could be discovered and developed in hitherto unexpected quarters.

This change in the way in which work could now be drawn up and distributed to those available for employment had massive repercussions. The new flexibility on offer favoured change on a scale that would have been impossible in the older societies where individuals were locked into stereotyped roles. The greater scope for personal initiatives allowed innovations to flourish. Workers found the best way to use their trade skills to advantage. Productivity shot up and a standard of living was reached that was incomparable with anything seen before.

The arrival of universal education increased the basic employability of people and so prepared them for whatever changes might take place in the demands of work. That single factor brought about conspicuous economic benefits that remained unqualified for a long time.

But in due course universal education produced a number of unwanted side effects. In the first place, the later age of entry into work, which is the price paid for extended education, meant that suitability for any given job had to be presumed. And it was often presumed wrongly. Young people would follow a course of learning without much insight into the reality of the demands of the work for which they were being prepared, whereas, before, the suitability of an apprentice had been proved before any qualified person was appointed.

A second difficulty arose from the widespread nature of what was on offer in training and education. Much of the attraction of the apprentice tradesman lay in the scarcity of that skill. As more people became eligible for jobs, employers would find that eligibility was not enough. In theory, any one of a large number of candidates might prove suitable.

A third difficulty arose from the changing nature of work. Up to a century ago, all jobs were well defined and well understood. They had job titles that conveyed, both to the job holder and the wider world, exactly what was expected from anyone in that job. No communication problem arose until the formal boundaries of jobs began to break down. With the rapid advances in technology and strategic thinking, employers placed a growing emphasis on versatility and team-work. This shift in priorities was to affect operator and management levels alike.

The sum total of all these changes has brought about a peculiar situation. Increasingly well-educated and trained job-seekers are applying for positions, the exact nature of which they find difficult to comprehend, while employers are considering the credentials of large numbers of possible candidates whose suitability they find hard to assess.

The situation can be likened to a group of people trying to find suitable partners in a dark room. Each is hoping to switch on the light, not knowing that the switch lies in a room outside.

The contention before us is that while the last and most radical phase in ways of distributing work, based on acquired individual skills and qualifications, has helped to raise the standard of living to new heights, that formula for the expansion of jobs and opportunities is coming to an end. Education, in supplying literacy and numeracy, is no longer offering a rare skill. In theory, people are better prepared than ever before for whatever varieties of employment lie ahead. And yet progress has removed the old certainties about future prospects that age, gender, race and traditional apprenticeships could offer. There are fewer signposts. People gather in increasing numbers wondering which road to take.

A new language will be needed if the changed requirements of versatility and team-work are to be fully met in this modern age and if the ideas that lie at its heart are to be fulfilled.

2 *The qualifications mystery*

The general realization that skills and talents were unevenly distributed and could not be deduced merely by taking account of the general classification to which a person belonged had enormous implications for employers and employees alike. For employers it opened up the field of personnel selection; for employees it held out the prospect that they could better themselves by improving what they had to offer so that boundless vistas beckoned. The encouragement of learning was in the interest of both parties.

The great leap forward in wealth creation and prosperity throughout the nineteenth and twentieth centuries owed much to the consequences of spreading education and training. Work could now be organized to take account of the skills available. Decreasingly, employers took on general hands — the lumpen prolateriat that figured so prominently in some contemporary writing. Increasingly, employers looked for workers who could offer specific trades or, failing that, whose broadly balanced education rendered them good prospects for a miscellaneous range of responsible jobs.

The most sought after candidates were those who could score on both counts. The scramble of employers to find these most employable of people and to place them in key places in organizations had a major bearing on the pace of development, the rate of change and the success of enterprises.

Who are the elite?

It is often the case that everyone agrees about objectives; the disagreements arise about exactly how they are to be achieved.

During my early days in industry, when engaged in industrial fieldwork in preparation for a higher degree, an interesting dilemma was brought to my attention. The matter came to the fore in ICI, at the time the largest manufacturing company in the United Kingdom.

ICI placed a high premium, as befits a capital intensive process industry, on recruiting the most talented and well-educated staff. For the chemical industry the best graduate chemists are its life blood. Finding the most suitable candidates engages the seekers in what is known as the 'milk round'. This involves regular visits to what are considered the most advanced departments in the top universities in order to project the image of the company, to encourage applications, to interview the possibles, and so from a very large initial field to contribute to the drawing up of a short list from which, hopefully, the high fliers will be selected.

The correct identification of the elite, along with, of course, their specifications, were key issues. Those with first class honours were favoured over those with lower degrees, while the most academically qualified with doctorates in chemistry were treated as being on the top rung of candidates. In line with that belief, a policy was formulated of looking for PhD chemists as potential factory managers.

This seemingly logical standpoint eventually ran into a barrier. These most eligible of candidates were found to include an undue number of poor performers.

It was explained to me that these setbacks in placement probably reflected some overestimation of the need for chemical expertise. The chemical reactions contained in most processes could, it was alleged, be written on one side of a blackboard. A knowledge of engineering might be equally important and perhaps had been underrated. So it was that the company began to turn with some, but by no means overwhelming, advantage to chemical engineering — a subject viewed by chemists as akin to engineering and by mechanical engineers as akin to chemistry.

The lesson of the initial failure to relate the real demands of the job to the qualifications demanded began to sink in. It resulted in a shifting of the goal posts. The desired qualifications were reformulated. A more liberal view began to be taken of the sort of person who might become the manager of a process industry. The problem now became one of how to pursue a more liberal policy without dropping standards.

One undoubted merit in setting out very demanding standards of entry, whether on academic grounds or otherwise, is that it restricts the field. Without such restrictions a firm risks being flooded with applications. Separating the promising from the unpromising becomes a formidable task in itself. Under such pressures firms are liable to be distracted by peripheral factors, to attach undue importance to neatness of application, or whatever significance they read into handwriting, until finally they begin to despair of handling the operation efficiently.

The story about the PhD chemists illustrates both the practical advantages of restricting the field of entry — there are fewer to consider; and the disadvantages — the most promising candidates may be missed. Cultivating a very large field from which talent can be drawn must be a better strategy in principle. The practical difficulty is how to reduce the field efficiently and how to decide who is worth interviewing.

Getting to the short list

Once firms relaxed certain exaggerated requirements of entry, they had difficulty in coping with the consequences as the floodgates opened to aspiring candidates. It was but a short step to subcontract the whole business. With education systems turning out an increasing supply of eligible candidates, recruitment consultants came into their own and offered to make an immediate contribution by lessening the sorting load. Unburdened from the now difficult task of separating the wheat from the chaff, key managers could now confine their attention to the short list.

Experienced recruitment consultants shifted the emphasis away from academic record as a measure of ability and more towards a candidate's record of achievement. External senior appointments demanded someone who was a proved success in a similar industry and had exactly the experience required. At times, the requirement could be carried too far.

On one occasion *The Times* carried an advertisement for a manufacturing manager for an explosives factory in Venezuela. The appointee was expected to be a well-qualified chemist, evidently resident in the United Kingdom, with experience in all aspects of explosives manufacture and the possessor of fluent Spanish. If such a rare person were found and wished to migrate to Venezuela, it would seem almost churlish to wonder whether he might be any good!

As the qualifications for particular appointments became increasingly hard to meet, especially where specific industrial experience was demanded, it became clear that seemingly high performers were not easily extracted from their current positions. The sleuth work and the winkling out was now included in the range of skills of the successful recruitment consultant and gave rise to the growth of a new set of professionals who engaged in executive search. Such consultants operate largely on the telephone. With an extensive range of contacts and with some boldness in approaching those they do not know, they eventually find the person who possesses precisely the requisite credentials.

Track record, as set out on paper, now became the thing to look for. The point was not lost on the ambitious. People began to plan their careers solely to improve the look of their curriculum vitae. Often the CV grew in appeal in an unintended way. Some people, deciding to move on after encountering difficulties in the job, or through resentment in having being passed over, managed on the strength of their experience to secure a similar or even a better appointment in a competitive firm. A series of such mishaps could greatly enhance a CV and improve the superficial appeal of the candidate in the executive labour market.

On one occasion I had the privilege of knowing the executive who, according to newspaper reports, had received the largest golden handshake yet recorded in the United Kingdom. I had first met him when he was the sales director of a large firm. There he gained a reputation for promising what he could not deliver. Shortly after his dismissal he was appointed the managing director of a large group. In due course he found himself in a position of isolation from the rest of the Board and was persuaded to leave with compensation appropriate to his station. Almost immediately he found himself the Chairman of an even larger Group until forced to resign following disastrous financial results. The fellow himself had an engaging enthusiasm, a highly sociable nature and a proneness for arriving at big decisions on impulse and inadequate information.

Since then I have encountered several walking disasters who have owed the progress of their careers to the cultivation of a pseudo track record, which they can suitably embellish at interview.

Doing the right thing with disappointing consequences

The rationale for using a headhunter is that a very specific set of credentials lies at the heart of the matter. Some headhunters, one must accept, are skilled in discriminating between the real achievers and those who have moved on 'just in time'.

But still the basic problem persisted. As the years rolled by, I encountered a steady stream of top managers who complained that, while they had taken every care to find the right man and had spared no expense in the process, somehow the appointee, while obviously able, 'had just not fitted in . Specific complaints would be made which in themselves did not sound like convincing reasons for rejection.

An exception to this generality occurred in the case of new chief executives. In this area there were fewer complaints that the wrong appointment had been made. Of course, well-chosen chief executives are not expected to fit in. And, indeed, there was ample evidence that they failed to do so. But in cases such as these the outcome took a different turn. The team did not reject the chief executive; the chief executive rejected the team.

The train of events was usually as follows. A newly appointed chief executive officer (CEO) would take an early opportunity to meet the staff and reassure them that their qualities had been noted and were duly appreciated. The company, it was claimed, would carry on much as before, although one or two policy changes would in due course be put into effect.

After a few months had elapsed, the CEO would demand some early retirements from his close colleagues. At first this would be received with a measure of equanimity. Then alarm bells would begin to ring as first one then another senior colleague would be ousted until in the end hardly any members of the original team remained. Individuals who had been highly praised in earlier assessments would lose their jobs as readily as more pedestrian performers. A question which must be posed is what lies behind this commonly experienced occurrence?

Had the replacement members been able to display unrivalled credentials for the posts they were taking up, the changes might have been understood. A certain amount of adjustment is often necessary in the interests of progress. But instead the incomers were often no better qualified than the outgoing members.

What was evidently happening was that the CEO was choosing appointees with whom he felt comfortable. Indeed, it usually happened that the newcomers had worked with the CEO in the past. In cases such as these, conventional notions about credentials counted for very little.

But if credentials and qualifications were no longer the passports to career progression, what other factors had come into play? Did this phenomenon merely demonstrate the power of capricious favouritism? Was it all a matter of gaining entry to court — the key means of dealing with the sort of historical tyrants that figured in the preceding chapter?

Clearly, there is more to it than this. CEOs have usually earned their place in hard competitive struggle. While not immune to flattery, they are unlikely to be won over by sycophants and courtiers; for their priorities have everything to do with achieving their corporate commercial or organizational goals. How they relate to others in the pursuit of these ambitions is not easily appreciated from the outside. It is a subject that appears to be of critical importance. And it is one to which we will return later.

The rush for qualifications increases the problem

While qualifications and credentials may mislead, the fact remains that most people pin their faith on obtaining something physical that they can present to prospective employers. In many parts of the world an onrush of learners is to be witnessed, seeking career progression through 'better qualifications'.

Certainly, there are trades where that approach is not to be contested. Anyone who wants to become a plumber will undergo training leading to the possession of a certificate. In many places there is a general scarcity of plumbers, behind which lies the joke:

> What is the difference between a plumber and the Messiah? The answer is that the Messiah is more likely to come.

People may train to become plumbers or electricians to advantage; they may pursue vocational education at a higher level to become doctors or lawyers. But outside these specifically vocational areas, there is an ever-widening measure of uncertainty about what continued learning leading to higher qualifications can offer, let alone guarantee, in career terms.

Exceptions to the rule highlight the mystery

At some of the highest levels in industry and commerce, qualifications are conspicuous by their absence. The tycoons of recent industrial history in Britain, including such names as Tiny Rowland, Sir Terence Conran, Sir Clive Sinclair, Robert Maxwell, Sir James Goldsmith, and many others, reads like a roll call of those who 'never made it', by either choice or shortcoming (usually the former), to a university degree. I believe a similar picture emerges in other countries. Even in ICI, where reputedly 'people get nowhere without a degree', John

Harvey-Jones, the company's most famous son, lacked a formal degree and entered the company in a comparatively humble position as a work study officer.

A good general education may be an asset for life, showing its value in many unforeseen ways. But one begins to suspect that when prerequisite 'qualifications' have no direct bearing on a given set of job demands or the career in prospect, a deliberate entry barrier is being set up by employers. Such a device will, they reckon, filter out applicants who lack the ability, intelligence or dedication to commend their general promise. Of course, if job seekers were to lack such qualities and were shunted into a programme which ultimately provided 'qualifications', their job prospects would be unlikely to improve.

The point has been brought home to me on a number of occasions in cases where large companies have provided generous facilities for employees to further their education. Such facilities are especially attractive to individuals who have been passed over for promotion and believe that a 'lack of qualifications' has been their undoing. After several years of study, they 'qualify' and their expectations of job progression are duly raised. They apply to attend an assessment centre. But the eventual outcome does little to advance their ambitions. Bitterness soon sets in. They feel they have been misled. Even though they may remain in employment, they fail to give of their best.

Where the unqualified progress and the qualified fail to progress, the paradox requires some explanation. Some important extraneous factor must have been left out of account.

One thing is clear. While learning away from work can be rewarding, the scope for learning within the work environment may be greater than people realize, even though the former is structured and the latter is not.

The hidden advantages of informal learning

How, then, should people equip themselves for work? The answer may lie through work itself, through the lessons it teaches, through what people learn about themselves and others. Like competing in the Olympic Games, the great thing is to have taken part. Unless people enrol for the event, they cannot win any races.

Given that some of the most successful performers in industry started work early, how and why they progressed is something of a mystery. The record is not one of unqualified success. Careers were often chequered. Having had the good fortune to have crossed the tracks of some famous industrialists by being, for a time, in the departments in which they had worked in their early years, I have observed their colleagues citing a range of strengths and shortcomings not unlike those that attach to us all. Nevertheless, the distinguishing feature is that those who succeeded seemed to have found their 'position'.

Here, one might take an analogy from team sports. If all the players on the field were to chase the ball at the same time the result would be chaos. A good team comprises players who restrict their activities so as to avoid diminishing the role of others but who play their own role with distinction. Not all positions require similar skills or even physiques. Establishing early on one's best position appeared to be not only the mark of the successful sportsman but of the successful industrialist as well.

In industry it is not easy to establish one's position, unlike team sports where positions are given a formal name. There are few ambiguities about professional titles, technical trades and managerial levels in a formal hierarchy. But these titles are inclined to obscure the real positions. The dynamism of a firm is often linked with its informal systems. That is what gives a firm its distinctive character. Outsiders will have difficulty seeing it but the successful players will understand. They know the position of the other key players, where they are stationed and to whom they may pass the ball to advantage.

As the years passed by in industry and I enjoyed the educational benefits arising from visiting a variety of firms, a general picture began to emerge. The formal language in which people engaged in discussing the qualifications of candidates or the job titles for which they were being considered seemed like a mask. The, often unobserved, reality lay underneath.

It was not until the opportunity arose to conduct research at Henley over an extended period on the functioning of management teams that light began to shine. The obscurities were removed and the shape of a hidden language was gradually revealed.

3 *Emergence of a team-role language*

Where the demands of a job are fully predictable and can be specified precisely, and where individuals can undergo a course of training that enables the skills required to be developed to the desired standard, the matching of people to jobs becomes a straightforward business. There is, however, one drawback: this is largely a vanishing scenario. It applies least of all in the world that executives inhabit. So volatile is this world that it is not unusual for the specific demands of a job to change even before a newly appointed executive has settled in, or for an appointee to start in a post without being fully aware of what the job entails.

The crunch question in the long run is not, therefore, what a prospective employee knows, or what specialist skills are possessed: what matters most, given a fair field of adequately qualified candidates, is how the chosen person is going to behave. That is why team-role language was first brought into being.

It was the uncertainties about individual behaviour, especially in the context of the working group, that had engaged my curiosity long before the opportunity for research appeared. And when the occasion presented itself at Henley, that same curiosity accounted for our persistence in pursuing our experimental studies of teams over a period that, from introduction to final exit, spanned nine years.

Henley College itself, set in a stately home by the Thames and claiming to be the longest established in Europe, had felt unsettled about the variablity in learning between its syndicates. These comprised 10–11 executives, carefully balanced in background, so that a wide range of skills and experience was available in each. The syndicates studied important issues collectively, drew on the testimony of speakers, explored other resources and presented their reports to the directing staff. Evidently the formula was successful. The 'members', as they were called, testified to their personal growth at the College. Many syndicates found the experience of collective learning so rewarding that they agreed to continue their association and would arrange a syndicate reunion dinner each year in London.

The problem lay with the exceptions. Some syndicates never gelled. At the end of the 'session', as each course was known, members were quite happy never to see one another again. The College had no idea why this should be so.

It is not my intention to repeat here an account of these studies which have been presented in my earlier book — *Management Teams: Why They Succeed Or Fail* — other than to present an overview of their conclusions.

However, before doing so, two salient points should be mentioned about the nature of the work. The first is that the investigation started with no preconceptions. The design of the inquiry was constructed in such a way as to enable the key factors to emerge. And it took a long time before they did. The second point is that the basis of learning hinged on acquiring an ability to make predictions about team performance. That has to be the ultimate test of any theory. Moreover, it may be contended, it is the only way forward in conditions where the miscellaneous nature of the material precludes unqualified comparisons, for every team is liable to possess some unique features.

The prediction of the outcome in the Management Game was made in a sealed envelope on the Monday morning, once the identity of the Chairman was known, and compared with the financial result on the Friday afternoon. The basis of the prediction rested on the scores from the battery of psychometric tests that all, or rather nearly all, the members completed. Additional feedback to the experimenters, once the exercise was over, came from the records of trained observers who were allotted one to each team.

To summarize the main finding briefly, what transpired was that particular individuals took on particular roles with the pattern of role balance exercising a crucial effect on the outcome. A poor balance would produce a poor outcome. Teams of able people would not necessarily produce favourable results since the balance might be wrong. On the other hand, a team needed able people in order to succeed. The composition of the team — a subject almost totally neglected by contemporary thought — therefore proved of crucial importance.

The types of behaviour in which people engage are infinite. But the range of useful behaviours, which make an effective contribution to team performance, is finite. These behaviours could be grouped into a set number of related clusters to which the term 'team role' is applied.

The continued evolution of team roles

The nine team roles now in current use are presented in Table 3.1. They differ in a few respects from the team roles first identified in the earlier Henley research. Two of the roles have been renamed, largely for reasons of acceptability. 'Chairman' has become 'Co-ordinator' and 'Company worker' has become 'Implementer'. Chairman was originally chosen on the grounds of factually referring to the role of the person in the Chair. In the end it had to be dropped for three reasons: its status implications were judged too high for younger executives; in the eyes of some it was 'sexist'; and it was liable to be confused with the title that could signify the head of a firm. 'Company worker', by contrast, proved too low in status, being especially resented by managing directors who were so described, and the word 'Implementer' was eventually substituted.

Inevitably, people objected to some of the other role titles. Terms supposedly more self-evident in meaning were preferred by some; for example 'Ideas person' for 'Plant' or 'Critic' in place of 'Monitor Evaluator'. Here, any advantage in greater ease of comprehension had its downside, being the risk of confusion and the loss of a proper understanding of the concept. True, a Plant will generate new ideas. So also will a 'Resource Investigator'. The latter is a different type of person, operating in an entirely different way, by borrowing and developing ideas in discussion rather than by originating them, and suited to a different type of job. The term 'Critic' is easily understood but the nuance is largely negative. The most positive aspect of the designated team role is one of balanced impartiality and considered judgement and this is where 'Monitor Evaluator' scores over 'Critic'.

There is one problem about the team titles that can never be adequately resolved; for while English is the most widely used international language, standard English does not exist. This is so even in the United Kingdom where, for example, a substantial dictionary has been published of English words as used exclusively in lowland Scotland. An additonal problem is that variations occur not only in working vocabulary but in the meaning and flavour of words commonly used. For example, in American English the term 'Plant' can have sinister implications, suggesting a management spy. One favoured alternative in the USA is 'Innovator'. However, Innovators require not only ideas but thrust. This latter quality is associated more with 'Shapers'. The dilemma, then, is whether or not to adopt the simple words that are part of everyday language in each culture

Table 3.1 The nine team roles

Roles and descriptions – team-role contribution	Allowable weaknesses

Plant: Creative, imaginative, unorthodox. Solves difficult problems.

Ignores details. Too pre-occupied to communicate effectively.

Resource investigator: Extrovert, enthusiastic, communicative. Explores opportunities. Develops contacts.

Overoptimistic. Loses interest once initial enthusiasm has passed.

Co-ordinator: Mature, confident, a good chairperson. Clarifies goals, promotes decision-making, delegates well.

Can be seen as manipulative. Delegates personal work.

Shaper: Challenging, dynamic, thrives on pressure. Has the drive and courage to overcome obstacles.

Can provoke others. Hurts people's feelings.

Monitor evaluator: Sober, strategic and discerning. Sees all options. Judges accurately.

Lacks drive and ability to inspire others. Overly critical.

Teamworker: Co-operative, mild, perceptive and diplomatic. Listens, builds, averts friction, calms the waters.

Indecisive in crunch situations. Can be easily influenced.

Implementer: Disciplined, reliable, conservative and efficient. Turns ideas into practical actions.

Somewhat inflexible. Slow to respond to new possibilities.

Completer: Painstaking, conscientious, anxious. Searches out errors and omissions. Delivers on time.

Inclined to worry unduly. Reluctant to delegate. Can be a nit-picker.

Specialist: Single-minded, self-starting, dedicated. Provides knowledge and skills in rare supply.

Contributes on only a narrow front. Dwells on technicalities. Overlooks the 'big picture'.

Strength of contribution in any one of the roles is commonly associated with particular weaknesses. These are called allowable weaknesses. Executives are seldom strong in all nine team roles.

and to risk the side effects. Familiar words are at least easy to understand and remember. But their real disadvantage is that they carry unwanted meanings and preconceptions that are difficult to shake off. Given that risk, my preference is for less familiar terms that can be imbued with their own specific meaning. That is why some foreign language editions of my work have retained the original English terms and have shunned their translation.

Perhaps the most significant of the changes introduced was the decision to add a ninth role, 'Specialist'. This role was added as a result of post-experimental industrial work. Its significance was brought home to me on two counts. The first was that in much project work a given form of professional expertise counted for a lot and could be ignored only at peril. (In this respect, the real life situation had not been altogether foreseen in the Management Game — the setting from which all our initial understanding had been derived — because pre-existing knowledge was not required.) The second cogent reason for adding the role to the existing eight was its recurring importance as an issue in career development. Certain questions were commonly asked. Should Sam Spencer, who had been making a singular contribution on Job A, be transferred to Job B in the interests of widening experience? With the wisdom of hindsight the answer would turn out to be No. Yet, in contrast, Gavin Grant, who could be more easily spared on Job A, would show commendable personal growth in making the job switch. The importance of distinguishing the valued Specialist from the valued Generalist has come increasingly to the fore as an important issue with which management needs to grapple when handling talented personnel.

The extent of such individual differences in predisposition towards each of the nine team roles was a matter that could hardly be ignored by those aspiring to make the best use of human resources. And yet the difficulty in judging the affinity of individuals towards each of the roles posed both theoretical and practical problems.

Identifying and developing team roles

People are inclined to be judged by what is visible about them. Gender, age and physical features offer leads. If such features fail to provide adequate information on the roles that people adopt at work, other cues are introduced. The most deliberate of these is uniform. In walking through a hospital the duties of each member of the hospital staff may be gauged accurately from what is worn. In other settings, where clothing is left to personal taste, the choice may still denote a person's role or rank or even occupation.

However, the roles that people take in a team are seldom evident at all from their features or general appearance. A person making a creative suggestion may look very much like one supplying information. A readiness to engage in dialogue is barely distinguishable from someone trying to take charge. With so much visual noise about, the correct signals cannot be read with any confidence. That is why when a group of strangers meet for a purpose so much time is spent in probing, in weighing up each other and avoiding getting down to real business. It may even be argued that such 'wasted time' is well spent; for in the course of these personal interactions, preliminary manoeuvres allow perceptions to be formed. From these, basic relationships can be established. Such a seemingly profligate use of time may in reality serve to increase the prospects of success.

The conclusions that people reach about each other, where there are few obvious cues, are made that much easier with experience because people exhibit certain regularities in their behaviour. They talk a lot or a little; they intervene when particular openings present themselves; their contributions assume one form or another. To the extent that idiosyncratic forms of behaviour are appreciated or rejected, individuals learn to steer a path, choosing roles adjusted both to their natural disposition and the social setting. Through such learning, a given pattern of behaviour evolves and settles down. People know what to expect from those they have seen at work over a long period.

Team role versus functional role

The term 'team role' refers to a tendency to behave, contribute and interrelate with others at work in certain distinctive ways. For practical purposes one needs to discriminate sharply between a person's team role and 'functional role', where the latter refers to the job demands that a person has been engaged to meet by supplying the requisite technical skills and operational knowledge.

The significance of the difference is that people appointed to a given job are likely to vary greatly in their team role. But their functional role is, or should be, exactly the same. Any criticisms levelled on the functional role of appointees will reflect adversely on training and perhaps on the inadequate way in which their job has been specified.

Any objections likely to be made on team role will reflect adversely on selection, though in mitigation it should be said that very few people know how to select for team role.

Since individuals with the same functional role, and who share a common background, may show a wide spread in team roles, the question arises why such differences should occur.

Such a question engaged our thoughts for a long time at Henley. Initially, we believed that the variation in contributions could be explained by fundamental personality differences. It is an axiom of science that phenomena should receive the simplest theoretical treatment and only failing that should more elaborate theories be developed. It was in this spirit that in the early days at Henley we used only two tests on the members who made up the teams: one being the Watson Glaser Critical Thinking Appraisal, a measure of high-level reasoning ability, and the other being the Cattell 16PF. The latter was a core personality inventory which, as its name implies, produced scores on sixteen personality factors or dimensions. In the early stages it seemed reasonable to assume that the CTA would yield a measure of ability while the 16PF would cover behavioural differences adequately.

That assumption was well upheld for one team role in particular — that of Plant, where a high score on the CTA and on a formula for creative disposition, using ten of the personality dimensions, proved a useful predictor of behaviour. Company Worker (later Implementer) could be predicted from a formula using six of the scales of the personality inventory, with the CTA having no obvious bearing. But as other team roles were discovered, it became clear that the two tests on their own, while providing useful leads, were not as predictive as we would have liked.

The team roles where scores on the 16PF had least bearing on behaviour were Monitor Evaluator and Specialist. The formula for Monitor Evaluator used only two scales on the personality inventory, though, fortunately, a good secondary predictor was a high score on the CTA, especially on its fifth component which dealt with an ability to think straight in dealing with controversial items. As indicated earlier, Specialist was a role we did not fully discover until the experimental work at Henley had been completed and perhaps the reason was that the Management Game did not really call for any specialist knowledge. However, when the role did come to the fore, we were not very successful in identifying on the personality inventory the factors typically associated with Specialist role behaviour. Indeed, it is doubtful if a predictor would have been discovered at all had it not been for a third test, which, after two years' work at Henley, we had thought fit to introduce. It was this test that refined the information derived from the first two tests and therefore justified the concept of a test battery as a predictor of team roles.

Predictors and overriders

The PPQ — its full name was the Personality Preference Questionnaire — was developed in the Industrial Training Research Unit at Cambridge by my able and enterprising colleague, Bill Hartston, who at the time was the current British Chess Champion. The PPQ comprised 50 pairs of names of celebrities in comparable fields. Bill's subjects recorded their preferences along with the reasons for making them. Each reason was then sorted into one of 20 construct categories to afford a frequency count over the range of categories. The construct distribution pattern was then used to supplement the data from the personality inventory. In effect, the PPQ became an additional predictor and in due course a link was found between certain construct patterns and observed behaviour.

A construct, it must be borne in mind, can be very important; it typically embodies a set of ideas and concepts about the outside world. In the language of some it corresponds with a philosophy, outlook or value system. People have very distinctive outlooks. While it is arguable that they have their roots in personality, it is undeniable that they are strongly influenced both by upbringing and interests. Whatever constructs are and however they come about, there is a robustness about them. They have a persistence in the way they influence behaviour.

The constructs of the PPQ proved more predictive of observed behaviour than scores on the personality inventory in the case of two team roles, namely Monitor Evaluators and Specialists; they were comparable as predictors in the case of Shapers, Plants and Co-ordinators; and they added marginally to the identification of the remaining team roles, apart from Resource Investigators, where they added nothing that could be detected as useful.

However, on a general point, personality and values (as embodied in the PPQ) often operate in conjunction. When they do so their combined predictive power is especially strong. Yet there were times when they were at variance with one another. For example, a person who stood out as a Team Worker on the 16PF might lack the distinguishing interest in people that one might expect to find from constructs on the PPQ. Or a very social set of constructs might be found in someone of introverted disposition. On this latter score, one reflects on many a great figure in the literary world who would live as a recluse yet write with the deepest insight about people.

When personality traits and constructs diverge, a more complicated picture arises. One of two principal outcomes is observed. The first is that the individual has failed to establish any distinctive team-role pattern. A Team Worker who has a minimal interest in people may be regarded as flat and insipid rather than as an asset to a team. A Shaper with low achievement orientation may succeed in aggravating people rather than driving them forward. Individuals whose traits and constructs conflict often have difficulty in establishing a clear team role either in their eyes or in the eyes of others.

The other contrasting outcome is that divergent traits and constructs can convey a wider range of team roles than any one of these measures alone imply. For example, Monitor Evaluators were discernible from the combination of high CTA marks, low achievement orientation scores on the PPQ, and low surgency (F scores) and high Shrewdness (N scores) on the 16PF. Some individuals displayed all the sangfroid and cerebral skills of the Monitor Evaluator, yet were atypical in respect of unexpectedly high achievement orientation. In these cases it was often found that an individual could switch from calm dispassionate analysis to a display of high drive and energy once a decision had been reached. What was being signified was not a limitation in any role but a wider repertoire than might have been supposed.

What in the end was available to us at Henley were three seemingly independent predictors. These yielded leads on personality, mental ability, and values and motivations. Different pieces of this battery were used to forecast the likely behaviour pattern of the various team roles. That concoction may sound complicated. The reality was even more complicated. What eventually came to the fore was a significant interaction effect between the predictors themselves. The personality factors predicted behaviour less well among the high scorers on the CTA than among the low scorers. In other words, there seemed evidence that strong mental ability can override personality. A comparable effect was found with the constructs on the PPQ. While these sometimes provided information of marginal value in the assessment of team-role behaviour, in the case of very pronounced scores they appeared to override the data generated from the other tests. So, for example, a pattern of strong subjective constructs allied with high achievement orientation would signify a Shaper mode of behaviour, even where the 16PF scores pointed in the contrary direction.

The existence of overriding factors did not stop at the measures within the test battery. Other overriders operated which had an observable affect on behaviour in the team. The first of these which came to our attention is what is generally known as Experience.

The lessons drawn from life

The occasion arose during the inquest on a team that had finished with poor results in the Management Game, very much in accordance with our expectations. What was unpredicted was the reason for the failure. The Chairman elected by the team appeared from the test scores to be a driver but dominant and arrogant and without any compensating talents to qualify him for the role. It was no surprise, then, when our Observer noted that one factor accounting for the disappointing outcome was the poor performance of the Chairman. However, the nature of his undistinguished behaviour lay in the opposite direction from that expected. Instead of dominating proceedings, the Chairman was criticized for his laxity throughout the exercise. So mystified was I by this report that I thought fit to interview him later and to ask why he had behaved as he did. The answer was that he had been spoken to earlier in the course by a member of the directing staff and asked to tone down his dominance of his syndicate. Evidently, the advice had carried over into the Management Game itself.

There have been many occasions when those I have interviewed have referred to some momentous event in their business lives which has had a lasting effect in changing their line and approach. All this has to be taken into account when we consider how any one individual arrives at a given type of team-role behaviour.

Two more factors have stood out similarly as intervening to modify team-role patterns. One we refer to as Constraints. Some have argued that behaviour is the best predictor of behaviour. In the long term that may be so. In the short term observed behaviour may mislead.

The essence of the matter is that people inhibit their natural behaviour or change its form to take account of immediate factors in the environment. If a boss is present, few people behave as they do normally. Of more concern is how candidates conduct themselves at interview. I have encountered numerous incidents where a secretary seated outside the interview room has made far shrewder judgements about a candidate than the interviewing panel itself after all its deliberations. The explanation is that candidates behave artificially in front of panels. Some of this behaviour is learned, especially by professional interviewees: in unconstrained situations the true person is revealed. This Constraint factor intrudes in other settings. It is present in assessment centres, where it has been observed as the goldfish-bowl effect, and is very liable to interfere with the value of the data derived. On the whole, extroverts tend to be overrated in such situations and introverts underrated.

The final overriding factor is one that we have deliberately set out to cultivate. It is called 'Role Learning'. Role Learning is what occurs when individuals participate in education on team skills. By recognizing the roles of others and by becoming aware of the range of roles that are available to the self, along with those that are not, people learn to modify their behaviour to take account of the situation. So it becomes possible to manage an association with others for whom an individual feels no natural affinity. These areas are explored further in Chapters 7 and 8.

My preferred model of the factors that determine team-role behaviour is given in Figure 3.1. I have used the model for many years and have

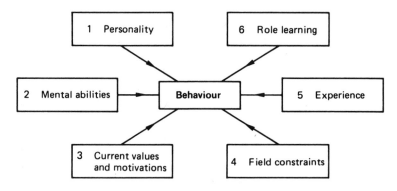

Notes:
1   Psycho-physiological factors, especially extroversion–introversion and high anxiety–low anxiety, underlie behaviour.
2   Nevertheless, high level thought can override personality to generate exceptional behaviour.
3   Cherished values can provide a particular set of behaviours.
4   Behaviour can depend on factors in the immediate environment.
5   Personal experience and cultural factors may serve to conventionalize behaviour *or* behaviour is often adapted to take account of experience and conventions.
6   Learning to play a needed role improves personal versatility.

Figure 3.1   *What underlies team role behaviour?*

never had occasion to alter it. Simple it may appear on a piece of paper; in practice it represents an enormously complicated process. What it means is that individuals eventually arrive at a stable pattern of association with their fellows based on a personality propensity, modified by the thought process, modified still further by personal values, governed by perceived constraints, influenced by experience and added to by sophisticated learning. To unravel the process that leads to some final feature of established behaviour would seem an immensely difficult task and is perhaps unnecessary where the aim is merely to take account of what those constants of behaviour are.

Role versatility versus role priority

The model on offer does, however, help to explain some of the idiosyncratic features of particular behaviour patterns. For example, one sometimes encounters a member of a political or religious sect with a set of acquired values who acts in a rebellious or defiant way towards outsiders, yet turns out to have an essentially mild and accommodating personality. The picture may be further complicated by the possession of a logical and inquiring mind which acts as a third force pulling in another direction. The consequential instability presents a problem if that individual moves in a wide world. Such a problem is found not infrequently among well-educated people where education may even add to the conflict. Any instability based on conflict means that clear team roles emerge slowly and indistinctly.

That does not, however, debar the possibility that the several factors underlying team-role behaviour can combine to facilitate role versatility; and so it is conceivable that a potential liability can be turned to advantage. For that to happen, the inner conflict that has been noted needs to be resolved at a conscious level. Thereafter, a foundation can then be laid for the development of a personal strategy, the requirements for which will be examined in Chapter 8. The price paid for any failure to resolve this problem is that the instability of the factors inpinging on behaviour will preclude the development of useful and adaptive adjustment. What will manifest itself instead will be neuroticism.

Where there is an absence of conflicting factors, behaviour will be simple and uncomplicated. A given team role will have clear priority over other team roles and will be recognized readily by colleagues. Such a person will gain rapid acceptance in a team if in possession of the requisite role, but will have difficulty in shifting from that role once the need for it disappears. So, in general terms, the advantage of simplicity has to be offset against the limitations arising from rigidity. Whether such a disposition is seem as an advantage or a disadvantage will depend on circumstances.

According to those factors that underlie behaviour, people may be pre-eminent in a certain team role or they may be versatile. But it is difficult for them to be both, unless they work at the challenge.

The varied processes by which team roles are formed help one to understand why one should resist the depiction of team roles as stereotypes. Stereotypes promote rigidity of attitude and behaviour. It is certainly true that a certain type of set behaviour may fit a person perfectly for a position and then the tendency to treat a team role as a stereotype would cause no particular problem. But for most positions the possession of a range of team roles is an asset. Stereotyping would obscure the fact that mature individuals use a limited repertoire of team roles in a flexible manner to fit the needs of a given situation.

A language in common use

Leaving aside some of the complications noted above, the basic language of team roles is well established among management educationists, thinkers and strategists. One might say the form of measurement is almost incidental. Certain test constructors have preferred to develop their own team-role categories which mainly vary in title from those first established at Henley. In other instances I have given personal help to firms operating in the psychometric field by devising formulae, based on their own test material, that are indicative of team roles, as with the Birmingham firm of Personality Assessment Ltd, and Saville and Holdsworth, now one of the largest firms of occupational psychologists in the world. A carefully argued paper by Professor Peter Saville — 'Personality Questionnaires; validly maligned or vital human resource tools?' — provides an elegant validation of the team-role concepts based on the Occupational Personality Questionnaire.

The extraction from psychometric test material of a disposition towards certain team roles enables executives to develop clear expectations about the potential contribution of a candidate. In other words, complex data processed to appear in a simple form is often preferred to scores on multi-dimensional tests on which it is difficult to take an overview.

What has emerged along a broad front is that the clusters of behaviour — to which the term 'team role' is applied — are now widely recognized by leading practitioners in industry. Methods of extracting and compiling data to arrive at the personal role profiles of individuals may vary between them. What matters in the long run as much as anything is how the team-role profiles are used once the information has been collected.

4 *The eligibility versus suitability issue*

How is it that one person fits well in one job and a second person fits better in another? Over the years it became increasingly evident that the issue had something to do with team roles. A Plant/Shaper would be a complete misfit in a job in which an Implementer/Completer might thrive, and vice versa. It all depended on the job demands.

That realization prompted me to search for a new language for analysing jobs, one that would meet expected service needs in conventional terms and yet would fulfil a secondary purpose in lending itself to the depiction of the team-role shape of the person who might best fit the crucial job demands. The research and development embodied in this mission went on for many years, first under the auspices of the Industrial Training Research Unit and later in our own office once the financial support for that research had ceased. But, after many research and development trials in the field, the point was eventually reached when the goals of this endeavour were broadly met and where the specification of a job could be translated by computer transformation into a team-role profile, and a computer search could identify an individual whose shape most closely corresponded with the shape of the job.

It was then only a matter of time before management was faced with a perplexing and important decision. What happens when someone technically ideal for a given job is computer assessed as unsuitable and someone ineligible on technical grounds is recommended as ideal?

This is the sort of puzzling dilemma that computers sometimes pose. But after a while the thought occurred: is the computer behaving absurdly or is it forcing us to question premisses previously taken for granted?

In all probability I would have suspected some strategic error in the programming of our system had I not stopped to reflect on a recurring experience. It was one that would rear its head as a self-evident oddity until one was bound to observe that the phenomenon occurred with a certain regularity. Of course if oddities become predictable, they cease being oddities.

The experience, to which I refer, relates to the filling of a job. Whenever a new position is being created in a firm, the immediate boss, possibly in conjunction with others, will set out a person specification to match the job's demands. As we noted in Chapter 2, certain qualifications are usually specified on the presumption that, by so doing, standards will be protected. Once the finishing touches have been put to the document, a moment's reflection is liable to draw the following comment from the boss:

> Mind you, if those qualifications had been demanded for my job, I would never have been shortlisted.

Since some of these people 'who would never have been shortlisted' were proven successes in their jobs, the implications need pondering upon. It implies that, when positions of responsibility become vacant within a large firm, the supply of good internal candidates may be greater than is generally recognized.

A failure to spot a particular talent may derive from the fact that employees are engaged in jobs which place a premium on team roles that differ from those that would naturally be adopted. For example, a medium-sized engineering firm had suffered from small but increasing financial losses for several years due largely to the continued production of an obsolete product. The lack of any dynamic entrepreneurial spirit was very evident in the top management. It was therefore a matter of some surprise to me on visiting the firm to read in the town's evening paper that a supermarket in the town centre had just been taken over by a successful local businessman who had made his money in developing cold-storage warehouses; and to be told by my informants that this mystery man was none other than a cost clerk currently employed in the firm I was visiting. The cost clerk turned out to be a Shaper/Resource Investigator currently acting as a Completer/Implementer. His undetected role characteristics were being used fruitfully outside the company.

Even if talents are detected, the discovery may come too late to make the fullest impact on the firm.

The following are two examples encountered during the course of my industrial travels.

A large corporation was looking from within its staff for a few key leaders who could guide it in the future. With the benefit of a battery of psychometric tests that had been designed to measure calibre, one promising individual emerged who was head of the computer department. Simon Starr, long recognized as someone with outstanding mental ability, had found himself drawn into the computer world where his strengths could find a suitable outlet. But what set him apart from so many others in his field were his favourable mentions in his annual assessments as a good manager. For some time Simon had agitated for a more challenging job, so that now, with the new evidence available, top management gave renewed thought to his career development. Simon was keen to get into marketing. But he had no background. It was argued that he could not therefore take up a senior post in this new field. The only possibility was to slot him in at some intermediate level where he could pick up experience. However, computer experts are well paid and Simon had reached the top of his salary grade. Should he be made accountable to a nominated marketing executive, he would be reporting to someone lower in both salary and status. After reflecting on the difficulties, the company decided to leave Simon where he was on the grounds that 'changing horses in midstream is not a practical proposition'.

Another large corporation had a great deal of capital tied up in its process operations. Fittingly, the company realized that the calibre of its shift managers was one of the keys to its success as a manufacturing unit. In order to assess what type of person made the ideal shift manager, a reference individual was chosen. Mike Model was originally a blue-collar worker who had come up the hard way. Mike not only ran the plant more efficiently than any predecesor but he was an inspiring leader of men. So enthusiastic were his senior colleagues about him that I suggested it might be useful to ask him to undergo the calibre tests. 'It's impossible', I was told: 'He's retired.' 'But you talked as though he was a recent discovery.' 'So he was, although he'd been here most of his working life. After his promotion he held the job for only three or four years. Then Mike took advantage of an early retirement package. He's now taken a job in another firm.'

Four important quadrants

The problem with Simon Starr, Mike Model and our cost clerk was that they were presumed ineligible for jobs for which they might have been considered. They were ineligible but suitable.

There is another group of job holders who fall into the diametrically opposite quadrant. They are eligible but unsuitable. Their qualifications equip them perfectly for the jobs they hold. But their performance is inadequate. I can scarcely remember any large or medium-sized firm with which I am familiar where there was not at least one person who fell into this category.

What may seem an anomaly to others is less strange to us. At one time we ran a research project in the Industrial Training Research Unit at Cambridge which examined the differences between high performers and low performers in jobs for which the subjects were equally well qualified. It soon became apparent that the entry criteria (necessary for securing the job in the first place) were totally unrelated to performance criteria (the distinguishing features by which excellence could be assessed). We might even say that there is no prior reason why a candidate who is eligible should be suitable. The particular features of these evaluations are shown in Figure 4.1.

Taking eligibility and suitability as independent dimensions, a two-by-two table can be constructed. From this, two further quadrants present themselves for evaluation. One deals with people who are eligible and suitable, seemingly an ideal category. The second encompasses an impossible-sounding category of people who are both ineligible and unsuitable. The four categories, along with their outcomes, are shown in Figure 4.2.

Eligibility *versus*	**Suitability**
Entry criteria	**Performance criteria**
1 Qualifications	Aptitude
2 Relevant experience	Versatility
3 References	Assessments
4 Acceptability at interview	Role fit with those adjacent to job

Notes:
1 People may compensate for lack of aptitude by seeking recognized qualifications. But aptitude usually wins through in the long run.
2 Experience sometimes serves to channel behaviour down a particular path when what matters here is a wider range of behaviour.
3 References commonly distort the merits of candidates, whereas assessments enable individuals to be compared on the same yardstick.
4 Those who impress at interview are not necessarily the easiest to work with.

Figure 4.1 *Why the most eligible for a job are often not the most suitable*

	Expectations on outcomes	
	Suitable	Unsuitable
Eligible	Ideal fit	Poor fit
Ineligible	Surprise fit	Total misfit

	Observed outcomes	
	Suitable	Unsuitable
Eligible	*Disappointing* Ideal candidates move to greener pastures	*The real problems* The poor fits are reluctant to move and become difficult
Ineligible	*Surprise fits perform surprisingly well* In the job by accident, contented and staying put	*No problem* Total misfits leave of own accord

Figure 4.2 *Eligibility versus suitability (the placement dilemma). A comparison between expectation and outcome*

Emancipation into management

The question that immediately comes to mind is how it can happen that ineligible candidates are appointed to any given position. The answer in many cases is by accident.

Let us take the case of the 'ineligibility' rendered by prejudicial discrimination. That was the lot that befell women throughout much of the Middle Ages, for they were confined to ancillary jobs or, in the case of patrician women, were excluded from any significant jobs at all. But then an event occurred that threw the system. The Crusades took the nobility to war. In the event, this seems to have had a beneficial effect on university education, if I may cite my own university, Cambridge, and especially my own college, Clare. The facts show that several of the colleges founded in the fourteenth century, when university education expanded rapidly, bore the name of women. In the case of Clare College, the college crest shows the tears of Lady Clare surrounding the shield of her fallen warrior husband. With the loss of a patrician crusader, someone had to manage the estate. This must have created a conflict of options. Women were debarred from management, being brought up to spend their time in such gentle pursuits as sewing and tapestry work. On the other hand, commoners were deemed unworthy to take over the management of the estates of the great families. One of these two undesired options had to go. Given the choice, it was the fair sex that gained the opportunity. Some of the most important educational and charitable foundations in the Middle Ages were founded by women, nearly always due to the untimely deaths of their husbands. These ladies were rendered eligible for management by the deaths of their spouses. Their deeds proved that they were suitable for the roles that society normally denied them but which fate had thrust their way.

Women are not debarred from management in the age in which we live, but the interruption of careers for family reasons, or entry into positions with limited career prospects on the part of those contemplating early marriage, reduces the numbers who can compete effectively for the top jobs. A rider is that those who do compete often need to make a bigger leap than men. As in the Middle Ages, some of the most successful leaps into top positions on the part of women I have known, whether personally or more remotely by reputation, especially in smaller and middle-sized firms, have been assisted by early widowhood, often allowing them to take over the mantle of the deceased husband.

Widowhood is a chance factor that can create opportunity. But other chance factors can have a similar effect allowing hitherto unsuspected talent to emerge.

One such case came my way in my capacity as Chairman of Cambridge Product Innovation, a small company that helped large firms to invent and develop new products suitable for their business. As it happens we had occasion to meet a very large engineering group whose business was closely tied up with major defence contracts. These had been cut drastically due to the ending of the Cold War.

The company was seeking new business opportunities and products and after prolonged negotiation arrived at our premises. The party comprised three people of whom one was a woman who bore the title of Contracts Manager. Her presence was something of a surprise as the company had very few female executives. Since nearly all the senior managers were graduate engineers, we presumed that she herself must be a qualified engineer but when the drift of conversation suggested otherwise we hypothesized that she must be a lawyer, for she was very evidently on top of her job. When that hypothesis was also discounted, curiosity extracted the true story. Originally she had worked as a secretary to a senior executive. One of her duties was to type contracts. Her boss, on reading one nicely typed contract, expressed pleasure with the result, only to be told: 'Well, I think it sounds rubbish.' The secretary with the critical mind explained her objections to the content and wording of the document. On so doing she was invited to reword it, which she did. Her boss was pleased with the result and when another contract came up in an adjoining department suggested that she should take a look at it. As a result of a further useful contribution the new post was created for her and she filled it with distinction.

These examples have focused on women because women have in the past so often been 'ineligible'. Men of course can be equally 'ineligible', and perhaps even more so. The most extraordinary instance of male ineligibility was quoted to me in a seminar I was conducting in Johannesburg. After making the general point about individuals who were ineligible but suitable, one seminar member quoted a case from his own firm, as follows:

> My company is one of the biggest retailing chains in the country. Currently we have a fashion director who is rated the most successful we have ever had. Before his present appointment he was the manager of the butchery department. What happened was this. The previous fashion director fell ill and went into hospital. As he was expected to return, the post was held open for him but as time passed his absence created various administrative problems. Our unexpected newcomer was invited by the managing director to come into the department in the first instance merely to sort out the peripheral managerial problems. Later he advised the managing director that, as the chances of the fashion director returning were extremely low, they ought to advertise for a replacement; and he was invited to draw up a specification of the job for the purpose of initiating the recruitment process. Several candidates were seen but none seemed ideal. Meanwhile, the staff of the department reported favourably on their temporary boss. The decision was made to advertise later after the Christmas break and

in due course the recruitment process was set in motion again. The managing director was not greatly impressed with any of the new candidates and on hearing even more favourable reports about the 'temporary' boss declared to the former butcher: 'Well, you had better carry on.' It was a decision management never came to regret.

The idea of a butcher becoming a fashion director may sound absurd by conventional standards. As it happened, I had already come across a comparable transformation of a butcher's career, when engaged earlier in my career in a job creation programe in the United States. Community Progress Incorporated was situated in New Haven, Connecticut and had undertaken a human renewal programme focused on an area of hardcore unemployed. The West Street Skill Center, where I worked for a time, had a comprehensive plan for handling those it fostered: assessment, training, counselling and placement. Every newcomer has his skills or, more usually, his deficiencies assessed at an early stage. Since most of the enrollees had personal problems as well as skill deficiencies counselling played an important part in the Center's activities.

One case that received considerable help was that of a butcher named Joe whose business had begun to fail when supermarkets took over more and more of the meat trade. At the same time his marriage broke up. It was then that Joe decided to end his life by driving his car at speed into a buttress on the turnpike or motorway. He failed in that, too, and was so crippled that he was eventually classified as a quadriplegic. A quadriplegic butcher might seem to be ineligible for any demanding occupation. But Joe was revealed, through aptitude tests and interview, as an energetic, intelligent and highly social person who loved meeting and interacting with people. The solution to his rehabilitation was to try him out as a telephone life insurance executive. Since he could not pick up and dial a telephone, some special apparatus was constructed. Once contracts were ready for signing, Joe would be driven to the newly signed-up customer by an assistant. Joe was a natural salesman and eventually won his company's award as the top East Coast salesperson of the year.

When ineligible people turn out to be suitable, we refer to a 'surprise fit'. In one section of our computer programme, Interplace, we have set out to find surprise fits from among large numbers of employees. Some of these discoveries have been launched on new career paths. However, the numbers are small and one is forever liable to encounter objections from those who express the view that time is better spent seeking candidates who are eligible and suitable. Those, supposedly, are the ideal fits.

Paradoxically, it has been our experience that ideal fits are not always ideal. An individual who is very well qualified for a particular position and who performs excellently in it is inclined to move on, often after a short duration in the job. There appear to be two prime reasons for this. The first is that the appointee may not feel stretched and new challenges soon beckon. The second reason is that an appointee in an ideal job is building up eligibility for an even bigger job. The net effect is that appointees, who have often been recruited at great expense, use the job as a stepping stone as they move on to higher things. This is where surprise fits score. Surprise fits congratulate themselves on being where they are and feel the job a constant challenge. Moreover, being ineligible for other senior jobs outside the firm in their particular activity, they are less inclined to look for greener grass over the other side of the fence.

Special problems among the unsuitables

Just as surprise fits may prove a better long-run prospect than ideal fits, so also a parallel paradox appears among the unsuitables. The eligible and unsuitable usually present a bigger problem than the ineligible and unsuitable.

The ineligible and unsuitable constitute those who are clearly in the wrong job. They have often come about as temporary appointments, sometimes as fill-ins following a crisis. When they don't work out, few tears are lost. Both the appointee and the appointer recognize the position. The misfit leaves. There is seldom any hassle and life starts anew with no bad feelings on either side.

It is altogether a different case with the eligible and unsuitables. A failure represents a serious setback in a chosen career path. Evidence that a person is unsuitable will be taken as a personal slight and will probably be rejected by the person concerned. Where the vocabulary of team roles has never taken root, it may be difficult to explain why a person so eminently well qualified for a job is unsuitable. The rejected individual may see no other options ahead. Vigorous self-defence is the only strategy left and that almost certainly means that a counter-attack can be expected. The attempt to shift a person who is eligible and unsuitable is likely to result in a great deal of unpleasantness all round.

Because the eligible and unsuitables pose such a difficult problem, the common response from management is to let sleeping dogs lie. A situation may then come about where almost everyone recognizes the reality of the mistaken appointment apart from the individual in question. In consequence, many a company lives with an inherent weakness that no-one is prepared to do anything about. That is why in order to avert risks of a possibly enduring nature it is a wise precaution to check first on the team-role fit between the person and the job, and the team the person will join, quite apart from a check on a more general set of abilities.

A case for backing a suitable

Once it is established, both from self-reporting and from observer assessments, that a person has good affinity for a team role or set of team roles, the information may be stored and retrieved as required. So also, the demands of a job can be assessed and it is then technically possible for those demands to be turned by computer transformation into a person shape. The next stop is to computer search the data bank of assessed people for someone who best matches the profile of the job. The search is based on suitability not eligibility. It has been my contention, contrary to the popular view, that, in the case of internal appointments, there is little point in taking eligibility into account in the initial sifting. It is up to management to decide who is eligible and who is not. A candidate who would not normally be considered eligible can have his or her eligibility improved by carefully planned training and prepared experience if the claims of the candidate justify the effort.

A good example of this approach was recently provided by British Nuclear Fuels working in conjunction with Marsden Consulting Associates. The Company decided in pursuit of a total quality management programme to appoint a Quality Co-ordinator. Nearly all its executives had been assessed under the Interplace system and their team roles, along with the assesment details that gave rise to them, were included in a large data bank.

Once the job had been specified and rendered in a form compatible with the data in the bank, a computer search was made for the most suitable executive. The nominated candidate proved a surprise, being personally unknown to two of the directors, and being devoid of any experience of the field in question. The assessment material, however, reinforced the view that a very promising candidate had been identified.

Instead of discarding the candidate, the management decided to hold up the appointment and meanwhile offer the nominated person an appropriate training programme supplemented with some planned experience. In due course, after showing the promise that had been foreshadowed, the nominated candidate was duly appointed to the post in which he proved a considerable success.

A compromise strategy

The examples discussed above present the cause of the ineligibles. The citing of extreme, though true, cases may help to drive home the point that choosing the most eligible is not the best strategy in making appointments. That can be a formula for poor placements that are difficult and embarrassing to undo, while the formula also results in missing good people.

But in reality and everyday practice, some balance has to be drawn. One can hardly make a case for seeking candidates whose background and experience offer no ostensible claim on a job. What is recommended instead is that more scrutiny should be given to the semi-eligibles. By sifting through these, some very good candidates may be found. Even so, their lack of complete eligibility might prove a handicap. Candidates who are very suitable but only semi-eligible need to have this short-coming made up. This requires an imaginative approach. Much can be achieved through offering a programme of planned experience or by supplying specific training in areas where deficiencies might otherwise show up.

Perhaps the main thing to remember is that high eligibles are easily overrated, whereas suitables, who are good examples of the type, have a potential that is seldom fully recognized. They may not be fully useful at the immediate moment, but if they are nursed, developed and placed with due care and attention, there is every chance they will become valued contributors in a new setting.

Indigenous talent, discovered in this way, usually plants deeper roots and develops more loyalty to the organization that succeeds in combining personal recognition with the provision of actual opportunity.

An example of one job where computer analysis has suggested the need for a particular team-role profile and a candidate is given in the appendix.

5 *Coherent and incoherent role profiles*

Everyone who undergoes a form of team-role assessment will end up with a team-role profile, showing in rank order a degree of affinity with each of the nine roles. That does not mean, however, that people are clear about their self-image in their own eyes or that they project any evident role image to others. People engage in assessment exercises for no better reason than that they are asked to do so.

The difference in self-knowledge between those who are clear about their team role and those who are not is well illustrated by the contrast in approach between experienced managers on the one hand and, on the other, young graduates venturing into industry for the first time. The results are not quite as one would expect. There is in fact a widespread belief that young graduates are bold and impulsive in their general reactions, while older managers are cautious and considered.

A very different picture emerges, however, from the data available to us when team-role questionnaires are completed. The experienced managers stands out as decisive in terms of which team roles are played and which are not. The points available for distribution between the team roles are spread between a few favoured categories, while at the same time they avoid the good impression items. By contrast, young graduates, possibly imbued with the unrealistic notion of all-round excellence, spread their responses thinly and with hesitation, with the good impression items often being awarded more points than those that denote true team-role behaviour. In other words, the inner confidence of experienced managers appears to be derived from the clarity of their self-knowledge, whereas young graduate entrants to industry seem uncertain about their own identity. It is as though they are searching for a role that they have not yet found. The confidence displayed on the surface is often bluff.

The road to maturity

People need to know where they stand in relation to others if they are to succeed in establishing working relationships. That is why it is so important to help to foster a sense of personal identity in young people. Sadly, many an educational institution has impeded the development of this sense by favouring a conformism that embodies its chosen values. The more that image is cultivated, the more lost an individual feels when ultimately required to stand alone or to emerge into the outside world into an unfamiliar social environment. Oscar Wilde once observed: 'Conformity is the last refuge of the unimaginative.' It is also its training ground.

Those who rebel against the image and the rules of the institutions that raised them (and who often do well in later life) gain at least one compensation for any pain caused to themselves or others. They begin to discover who they are. The seeds of growth demand a consciousness of the self and its differentiation from the non-self. Adolescence becomes a journey that starts with rebellion and, ideally, proceeds through socialization to reach a new balance. The problem is that some hardly start on this journey, others take the first steps but proceed little further, while only a few travel the full distance.

In the development of team-role theory and practice, the switch between deriving team-role profiles from self-reporting, and in deriving them from a broader set of data, including the assessment of others, proved to be a step of great significance. In some ways it generated more trauma than the earlier approach. When individuals discover that their self-perceptions are at variance with the way they are perceived by others, they experience a shock to the system. Are they really as other people think or can it be that others have failed to understand them?

For some, a preoccupation with this conflict in information is eventually resolved by some positive decision about future conduct. It seems a mark of maturity in certain individuals that they can absorb information that others would find disturbing, and use it to their ultimate advantage.

But there is another type of maturity that has come to the fore and is denoted by what we term 'the coherence factor'. Coherence is a measure of the extent to which disparate information builds up to offer an integrated and meaningful picture of the personality. The source of this information usually comprises self-reporting, observer assessments and such psychometric test data as are available.

In everyday language, some individuals succeed in presenting a clear picture of themselves to the outside world, being a picture they are happy about and one that realistically represents who they are. However limited the skills they can offer the labour market, they have a way of rising above their disadvantages. Their literacy and spelling may be sub-standard. Or their lack of numeracy may debar them from any job that entails handling figures. Because they never mislead anyone in terms of what they can and cannot do, they manage somehow to find an appropriate role slot. They appear to be wanted wherever they take up employment.

Improvers versus non-improvers at work

The importance of character attributes, vis-a-vis the mere possession of skills, was first drawn to our attention when we were running The Industrial Training Research Unit in Cambridge. One of the research projects in the Unit had been conducted by a talented research worker called Eileen Sagar who had set out to investigate how it was that among the population of early school-leavers, most of whom had poor educational records, some made positive headway as soon as they left the world of education and started work. Eileen's method of investigation was to follow these school-leavers into industry, to identify who were the improvers and who the non-improvers and to differentiate between the two groups by means of what is called the 'critical incidents technique'. After supervisors had arrived at certain judgements about the young people, they were asked to enlarge on their assessments by citing some instances of behaviour. These volunteered instances were then classified into categories of similar items. This treatment of the material allowed a numerical count to be made of the typical behaviours of improvers and non-improvers (Figure 5.1).

Two things are evident from this figure. The first is that the differences largely revolve around behaviour and have little to do with technical skills or knowledge. A second point is that the qualities noted in the more effective group are not the mirror images of the qualities observed in the less effective group. Bad timekeeping is conspicuous among the non-improvers but good timekeeping, while a feature of the improvers, is ranked well down the scale of distinguishing features. More important than the absence of this shortcoming, for example, is the ability to seek work when slack, while versatility comes top of the list of features cited.

The overall picture of the school-leavers who were improvers is that

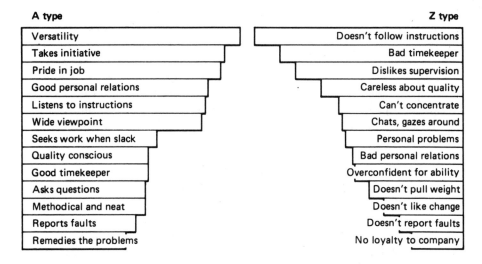

A type	Z type
Versatility	Doesn't follow instructions
Takes initiative	Bad timekeeper
Pride in job	Dislikes supervision
Good personal relations	Careless about quality
Listens to instructions	Can't concentrate
Wide viewpoint	Chats, gazes around
Seeks work when slack	Personal problems
Quality conscious	Bad personal relations
Good timekeeper	Overconfident for ability
Asks questions	Doesn't pull weight
Methodical and neat	Doesn't like change
Reports faults	Doesn't report faults
Remedies the problems	No loyalty to company

The leading factors volunteered by supervisors as characterizing based on forty-seven improvers (A) and forty-eight non-improvers (Z) type young employees starting work.

Notes:
1   Plus points in behaviour at work (A type) are not merely the converse of Z type behaviour.
2   Nearly all the points mentioned relate to character rather than skills.
3   Executives seeing these results declared: 'That applies to us too.'

Figure 5.1   *The maturity factor as it affects behaviour at work – the histograms represent frequencies. (After Sagar, Eileen,* The A–Z Study: differences between improvers and non-improvers among young unskilled workers, *ITRU Publication SY4, Cambridge)*

they were socially responsive and while properly mindful of instructions they would adjust their brief and role boundaries to ensure they were properly occupied when work was short. Even at a very junior level people found due scope for managing their own behaviour at work and the frontiers of the job territories within which they operated.

Junior, but poorly educated, improvers have their counterparts among the well-educated, well-qualified young candidates who also enter industry at a different level and of whom I have had far more experience. Most of those who make their mark through gaining early promotion appear to be no better technically than those who are passed over. Rather, it is their self-management and their ability to manage their role relationships with others that stand to the fore.

People with very coherent team-role profiles develop distinctive approaches to self-management. Being aware of what they are and what they are not, they learn to develop a strategy not only for operating in their favoured areas but for coping with the situations for which they are by nature unsuited.

Self-insight in the team generates coherent behaviour

The importance of developing self-insight in the team has come consistently to the fore throughout our stewardship of management games designed to offer an index of group achievement and therefore a measure of team effectiveness. That work had started at Henley with the Management Game, operating through a computer-based model of the business world (to which extent it favoured computer buffs); it continued after Henley with Teamopoly (a team game based on the modified rules of Monopoly) in which the luck element had been largely removed by making all purchases of sites dependent on initial allocation, auction, tender and negotiation, and by making provision for forecast cards for landing on sites so that financial outgoings could always be predicted; and finally the exercises continued with what was sometimes called Teamopoly II. This exercise retained the playing principles of Teamopoly I but cast the exercise in an entirely new form. Instead of buying sites the players bought two-dimensional building components, of various shapes, colours and sizes, that could be constructed to form object shapes. These could be sold to the market at given prices — the higher prices being obtained by the more difficult shapes. To finance these dealings money could be borrowed from the bank at high interest rates or by the sale of equity to the market on given terms. Teamopoly II had the advantage over its earlier version that it did not resemble, even superficially, an updated game of amusement, while the element of luck was reduced from small to zero.

All three exercises incorporated a common principle in team design. Participants were placed in unbalanced teams, that is to say, each group had a superfluity of strengths in some team roles and a deficiency in others. Most teams recognized this early on in the exercise but were inclined to shrug it off, soon becoming immersed in the specific task demands that they considered might lead them to victory. When the financial results were published at the end of operations the groups conducted their own inquests, appointing a spokesperson to present their analysis and overview to all participants.

Differing styles linked by a common maturity

The exercises outlined above have been conducted all over the world, both by myself and by Jeff Hayden, on behalf of Junior Chamber and, later, Management Teams International. We have worked both independently and together but, either way, one point has come to the fore about winning unbalanced teams. The best results have come from teams which developed well-informed self-insight and which took appropriate action in managing their style of operation. So, for example, Shaper teams that soon became aware of their problems avoided collective decisions. The members of the most successful of these teams recognized their preference for both action and autonomy: by so doing they would decide to act independently but in a concerted way in the discharge of their responsibilities. In contrast, successful Team Worker teams reached joint decisions on major issues, while their members worked in pairs at other times. Successful teams with highly creative members and a deficiency in Monitor Evaluators would appoint one of their number with the highest score in this role to act as adjudicator with the power to decide which idea should be adopted. A similar compensatory mechanism might be adopted by teams deficient in Completers. After recognizing a basic weakness the successful team would ask a member with the highest Completer role score to undertake responsibility for all delivery aspects of decisions and activities.

There were many other mechanisms and compensations that teams adopted to overcome a basic weakness. But those adjustments first needed to be triggered off by an awareness of the collective self-image and a desire to manage what was there effectively. A coherent self-image emerged, therefore, not only as an advantage for the progression of individuals but for the team itself. If a team fails to see itself as though from the outside, it cannot use its internal resources or regulate its activities efficiently.

Unbalanced teams with the poorest records fell into two categories. Either they failed completely to read the signs and carried on as though they were a team without problems; or they recognized the problems early on but acted fatalistically as though unable to change their fixed destiny.

Personal maturity has its counterpart in team maturity. The mature team knows what it is good at, realizes where its weaknesses lie, plays to its strengths and avoids engaging in activities where it cannot compete effectively. It will venture beyond these self-imposed parameters only if it succeeds in finding some compensating mechanisms. The mature team will cherish whatever abilities it possesses, even those of no more than of average order. But because those abilities are used to full advantage it will achieve superior results.

When weaknesses become allowable

Mature behaviour paid off well throughout the range of management exercises which we conducted over the years. Yet, as so often, a word in common parlance can be revealed as having several shades of meaning. A piece of behaviour may be recognized by observers as mature but what underlies it may give rise to debate.

For many, personal maturity implies a well-rounded person with a broad set of strengths and no evident weaknesses. To this model is ascribed a halo, the fitting headwear for any saintly person. In our position we were well placed to remove the halo and peer at what lay underneath. The reason is that we had available a large body of information based on either a set of psychometric data or the outputs from Interplace plus, in all cases, observations made during the exercise itself. What emerged did not accord with the halo view of maturity.

Mature people, if the word is to be maintained, were characterized less by the supremacy of all the most desirable attributes as by the coherence of their profiles. Their contributions were easy to recognize, they controlled the expectations of others appropriately and they did not set out to present themselves as supermen or superwomen. Nor were they. In a sense, most of the major contributors could be defined from the assembled data almost as much in terms of what they were not as what they were. What they were not did not present a problem because they never set out on paths liable to produce a disappointing outcome.

This observation raises the question of what we mean when we talk about a personal weakness. Some treat it as though it is a symptom of psychopathology and this is far from what I would imply. Weaknesses in individuals are sometimes deduced from psychometric tests for reasons that are largely technical so that their validity is open to challenge. Many tests are constructed in such a way that if a person is high on some attribute the same individual is bound to be relatively low on another. These are known as 'ipsative tests' and the ipsative effect is at its strongest with forced choice questionnaires. A low score on one attribute can be argued as being no more than an epiphenomenon of test construction and, in reality, means very little.

That thought was uppermost in our mind when we first observed high performers who were low scorers in certain areas. That was why in order to allow us a better lead on this phenomenon we moved, over the years, to a form of testing and assessment that did not involve forced choice. As a result of this journey we became better placed to answer two crunch questions. The first was whether the weakness really existed. The second was whether it mattered.

That so-called weaknesses did exist in high performers was eventually supported by examination of scores on tests from which forced choice was excluded along with scrutiny of observational material on performance in the exercise. Even talented individuals did not show up strongly in all areas of significant contribution. Philosophically, one began to see links between the animate world and the inanimate. No physicist would subscribe to the view that the perfect raw material did or could exist. If a material is exceptionally hard it may also be brittle or it may be prone to corrosion. This combination of the desired and undesired properties of given materials is a problem that has plagued the construction of nuclear power stations. Similarly, it may be argued, there is no perfect human material.

The clinching point, however, was the eventual discovery that a so-called weakness was often no more than the obverse side of the strength. Hence the Monitor Evaluator who possesses analytical powers allied with a capacity for objectivity is hardly likely to be an inspiring individual and, indeed, seldom was. Enthusiasm interferes with assessment. And enthusiasm is what is needed if others are to be excited by the prospects ahead. So also, Completers tend to be weak on delegating. Anyone intent on seeing a task through will not be happy about passing it on to another.

For each one of our team roles we discovered a corresponding weakness, and the more prominent the strength the more conspicuous the weakness was likely to be. That is why mega stars and mega politicians are almost as renowned for their quirks as for their talents.

That being so, we can now answer the earlier question raised: Does a weakness matter? In conventional assessment terminology, weak points are referred to as 'development areas', with the advice that they should be worked on so that they can be overcome. But my response is that if the weakness is the price that is liable to be paid for a strength, it does not matter at all, for it is a fair trade-off. The only proviso is that the person with that strength develops an appropriate strategy for managing that weakness. This issue will be covered in Chapter 8.

When allowable weaknesses veer towards unacceptability

A weakness which facilitates the strength associated with a given team role is called an 'allowable weakness'. These allowable weaknesses are set out in Table 5.1. Allowable weaknesses should not, of course, be corrected, for otherwise that might undermine the real strength. However, there are some associated weaknesses which may get out of hand and which detract from someone's team-role contribution rather than add to it. For example, a Monitor Evaluator may veer from being sceptical to becoming cynical. No one will wish to try out an idea on a cynic. A cynic is not dispassionate but is more akin to a Monitor Evaluator gone sour. These non-allowable weaknesses are also set out in Table 5.1.

Table 5.1 A thin line can separate some allowable weaknesses from unacceptable behaviour

Team role	Weaknesses	
	Allowable	Not allowable
Plant	Pre-occupation with ideas and neglect of practical matters	Strong 'ownership' of idea when co-operation with others would yield better results
Resource investigator	Loss of enthusiasm once initial excitement has passed	Letting clients down by neglecting to make follow-up arrangements
Co-ordinator	An inclination to be lazy if someone else can be found to do the work	Taking credit for the effort of a team
Shaper	A proneness to frustration, and irritation	Inability to recover situation with good humour or apology
Monitor evaluator	Scepticism with logic	Cynicism without logic
Team worker	Indecision on crucial issues	Avoiding situations that may entail pressure
Implementer	Adherence to the orthodox and proven	Obstructing change
Completer	Perfectionism	Obsessional behaviour
Specialist	Acquiring knowledge for its own sake	Ignoring factors outside own area of competence

Weaknesses are also non-allowable if they are acceptable in one context but are misapplied by being attached to the wrong team role. If a Team Worker is so diplomatic and sensitive to others as to be indecisive in many social contexts, that is to be condoned. But an indecisive Shaper offers the worst of both worlds: a display of aggression will generate opposition and antagonism without gaining compensation in terms of resulting action. In terms of allowable conduct, different standards need to be set for different people. Some will be permitted to act aggressively, others to be indecisive, while no-one should hold it against the Monitor Evaluator who is boring. Effective teamwork can never operate in a totalitarian culture where deviations from the norm are not allowed (a matter to be considered further in Chapter 10).

When allowable weaknesses operate alongside the strength of a recognized team role, they serve to enhance the team-role image. That combination makes for clarity of contribution towards which others can react appropriately. Those with coherent team-role images usually find it easier to establish themselves in a team.

Qualities that combine well

One theory about how it is that some individuals are more successful in their careers than others is that the former possess fitting combinations of personal characteristics while the latter display attributes that do not go well together. Here the position of the so-called weaknesses needs to be treated not in an absolute sense but in association with a cluster of other characteristics. For example, laziness would normally be considered a negative feature for any role. Yet one finds a few successful executives who admit to being lazy. Laziness will not exist in isolation in these cases but may be combined with judgement, a strategic sense and an aptitude for delegating. There will be time to talk to visitors because the work schedule is not overfull. The desk will be tidy with scarcely a paper upon it because 'my secretary clears things up'. The lack of preoccupation with incidental urgencies provides scope for the development of breadth.

There are some executives who are timid, shy and very poor at interpersonal communications. It might seem inconceivable to some that they occupy high places where they are well regarded. Yet beneath that mild exterior there lurks a great determination to succeed, to choose the route that will yield the best results and to take infinite pains to ensure that no factor that might spoil the plan is left out of account. The gap in social communications is often filled by others who strive to draw the person they respect into any cabal of key people. Such a person will at least end up communicating effectively with those who matter.

A person who is not well balanced may still end up with a coherent profile. What matters is that the self-image and the projected image cohere and that a strategy exists for coping with areas of deficiency.

But just as there are certain personal attributes that combine happily, there are also certain team-role pairings that go well together. A Shaper/Implementer possesses the drive to get things done, and the practical efficiency that goes with it. The image that is projected is of Action Man himself. Similarly, a Plant/Monitor Evaluator with known mental ability promises to be a creative intellectual with a capacity for good decision-making, ideally placed to develop plans and strategies that may pay off hugely in the long term. Clear and coherent profiles such as these lend themselves to easy placement.

Unusual combinations

Other team-role combinations, rarer and less natural, offer special opportunities but, equally, present dangers, particularly where the roles are inclined to pull against each other. For example, it is unusual for a person to have Shaper and Team Worker in the top two team roles, but it does occur. A person who possesses great diplomatic skills yet also proves a driving force can become an enormous asset to an organization. There is, however, a risk that such a person will be seen as two-faced by some, that is, as seeming nice but in reality being ruthless and therefore untrustworthy. Another risk is that the driving quality of the Shaper may be undermined by the Team Worker's proneness to indecisiveness.

That may well be the problem that beset Gorbachev. As a Team Worker he was ideally equipped to ingratiate himself with the Kremlin establishment and so rise to power, and subsequently to ingratiate himself with hardliner Margaret Thatcher, thereby contributing to the ending of the Cold War; yet he was also reputed to have courage and 'teeth of steel' at a level of which any Shaper would be proud. The indecisiveness which he showed on domestic and economic issues might therefore seem to be out of keeping. But they would not be out of line in a Team Worker. A true Shaper would have made decisions unhesitatingly, even if they had been wrong. The problem therefore arises that what would be an allowable weakness for a Team Worker is displayed inappropriately when it is the Shaper mode of behaviour that is required, in which case the weakness now becomes non-allowable and, in fact, a liability.

Complicated clusters present problems, yet they may still have a certain coherence. With good self-insight they can be managed to advantage. The same cannot be said for combinations of characteristics that offer no evident basis for the development of a viable personal strategy.

The typical referral

A substantial number of intended executives have difficulty at the start of their careers in industry in finding their right niche. Some never find their niche at all.

Over the years I have spent in industry, many young executives have been pointed in my direction and have been counselled by me after first taking a battery of psychometric tests. Many of these have been high fliers for whom a future career path within the firm is a matter of crucial importance, both for them and for their employers. But, along with this elite, I have seen many who have been referred to me in what is virtually an act of desperation. These would mostly be well educated and personable with copy-book backgrounds, destined, so it might seem, for higher things. The hitch would be that following each assignment negative reports would find their way back to management. In the end no-one would wish to retain them in some established position in their department. They would therefore be referred to Personnel for further consideration. In many cases the negative vibes had not reached the individuals themselves. Then I had the unenviable job of being the first person to impart the bad news. It is on this group of people, commonly described euphemistically in the United States as 'referrals', to which we should now focus attention.

One referral who comes to mind was someone we will call Donal. Donal was an entrant on a general management training programme developed by a large multi-national for young graduates of exceptional promise. Donal had been awarded first class honours in his subject from a prestigious university, while his energy and ambition had impressed all his interviewers. Nevertheless, on each of his training assignments the reports from departmental managers fell short of what had been hoped for. The problem was never quite the same so that management found it difficult to establish whether Donal had not been given the opening that he deserved or, for some reason, was merely an unfortunate appointment.

Donal consented to undertake a battery of psychometric tests as part of a general assessment exercise and he also completed the Team Role Self Reporting Inventory from which he emerged as a Plant. To be clever is a basic requirement for an effective Plant and here his academic record suggested support. But against this he achieved scores on some measures of mental ability below the norm for college graduates. Donal, in response, had disputed the validity of the tests on technical grounds and generally had a more favourable view of himself than the facts might have warranted. When asked how he thought he had performed on his assignments, he considered he had done well. A tentative mention of some adverse comments drew from him a torrent of criticism directed at certain middle managers to whom he had reported. Donal craved for an overseas assignment and eventually was placed in an associated company in the United States where his Englishness and drive created an initially positive impression. However, an undue time was spent in trying to renegotiate his overseas allowances and a stream of communications about him was for ever flowing backwards and forwards to Head Office. When he later returned to the United Kingdom with only a moderately satisfactory assessment, no one wanted him in their department.

The bulk of the objective evidence suggested that Donal was a hard-working Shaper/Implementer but needing discipline and structure to bring the best out in him. On the other hand he believed he was by nature a Plant/Monitor Evaluator with aspirations to become a Corporate Strategist. Perhaps the reality was that Donal was not a good example of any of the principal types of contributor who make their mark in management teams. He may be seen as a possessor of an incoherent profile.

Donal took up an undue amount of time from senior personnel and no fitting solution was ever found for his situation. Impatient with his lack of progress and still in possession of an attractive track record, he quickly found another company that he believed would be more ready to meet his ambitions.

Based on observation of a large number of special cases and of our experience with Interplace, we may conclude this chapter by advancing a working hypothesis: that individuals with coherent profiles are easier to place in jobs successfully than those with incoherent profiles, even if the technical skills of the former are inferior to those of the latter.

The significance of this hypothesis is that organizations have much to gain by recruiting a range of personnel who are good examples of the type. This policy may not go far wrong even if those recruited fail to match the presumed balance of demand at any given moment, for as conditions change they may slot quickly into place. But those with incoherent profiles at the outset may give rise to recurring problems for many years to come.

6 *Interpersonal chemistry in the workplace*

There are two ways in which team-role data can be used in the assessment of the suitability of candidates for any given position. One approach is to compare the team-role profile of the candidate with the demands of the job or, more precisely, with the demands as transformed by the computer into a team-role shape.

When it first appeared, this approach was radical enough. But there is an alternative approach that is even more radical because it breaks into ground that, to the best of our knowledge, has never been tackled before. The method involves discounting the job demands as such by assuming that the required technical skills and work attitudes are present, and focusing instead on the nature of interactive relationships that will result from the placement.

On the whole, the distinction that may be drawn between the two approaches is largely one of context. The diagnosis of job demands has paramount importance in the case of well-structured jobs where clear criteria exist on the behaviour associated with good performance and the failure to show that behaviour has immediate consequences.

Executive jobs at senior levels are governed by a different set of parameters. For one thing, the jobs are less highly specified: indeed the person makes the job, or so it is said. For another, success or failure is associated with a capacity for blending well with certain other senior managers.

So important is that latter aspect that new chief executives appointed from outside seldom settle down until they have introduced into key positions some members of the top teams with whom they have collaborated formerly. That a new leader should bring along his or her own cronies is a common source of resentment. But if the old cronies make that chief executive more effective, the subject needs to be treated with respect and a sense of inquiry.

Over a period of time, enough cases have built up of successful and unsuccessful relationships at senior level to allow a rough-hewn picture to emerge of the types that get along well together and the types that are prone to fall out. Executives who become embroiled in these issues are especially given to personal acrimony. All manner of faults and weaknesses are laid at the door of those with whom relationships have failed. It is a fair contention that, as in marriage, certain people are not made for one another. Much time and agony could be saved if that realization could be established at the outset before any damage was done.

When, very tentatively, we introduced a team-role chemistry module into Interplace we realized that we were boldly entering hitherto unexplored territory. What gave us the courage, or perhaps rashness, to carry on was the certainty that user reponses would be our tutor and would be bound to draw us back on the path to knowledge from which we may unwittingly have strayed. As it happened, our basic hypotheses did not prove to be that far out.

The eventual need was for elaboration rather than revision. Those complications we did encounter were mainly concerned with the impact of values. These can facilitate relationships normally associated with difficulty, or interfere with relationships otherwise likely to be harmonious. Research in this area is currently continuing. We hope that, one day, new modules will permit this area to be expanded. For the moment we have enough knowledge to lay down a few guiding principles, although there is every prospect that these may be elaborated in the future.

Single-role and multiple-role relationships

When two people interact in work they can respond to each other in a number of ways. They may relate solely in terms of their technical briefing and separate responsibilities for particular tasks. In that case it will matter little who the two people are. If they carry out their jobs in the way laid down and agreed, the result should always be the same.

Where work involves more dynamic interrelationships, the team-role shape of the two individuals will always have some bearing on what eventuates. If one person becomes aggressive and overbearing, the other may respond by being diplomatic and conciliatory, leading to an accommodation; but in the case of another, with a different team-role profile, challenge will be met with challenge and an unresolved argument may ensue.

When two strangers meet they may at first be reluctant to show their true shape but it will not be long before that shape emerges. The likelihood is that the primary natural team roles will be the first to appear. On the whole, people do not switch away from their favoured roles unless there is good reason for so doing. Hence, single-role relationships characterize the dealings of people who have not known each other for long or who have never had occasion to modify the way in which they are inclined to respond to that particular individual. People soon become typical of themselves in the eyes of others. 'The same old . . . .' will be the recurring phrase.

There are, however, relationships that are more intricate in nature. It is possible for someone to take on one role with a person in a social situation and quite another when it comes to problem-solving. For example, a Shaper/Plant boss may have a Team Worker/Monitor Evaluator subordinate. The primary relationship is of a directive nature with a Shaper controlling a Team Worker. But then the boss thinks of an idea that could have important consequences if everything proceeds as planned. But then it might not. 'Let me try this idea out on you', says the boss to the subordinate. The relationship has ceased to be directive. The Plant is talking to the Monitor Evaluator and is ready to receive advice.

This type of switch involves what we call 'multiple-role relationships'. These have to be learned over a period of time. In effect, one person will know how to deal with another in a variety of contexts. That responsiveness will itself be sensed so that mutual needs and benefits develop. A team of two, capable of multiple-role relationships with each another, can operate very efficiently in working arrangements, far surpassing a much larger team in terms of what can be achieved. That is why in career planning it can prove such a costly mistake for top managers to treat individuals in isolation. It is as though on a chess board the moves of each piece were considered only separately and the power of combinations was ignored.

The chemistry of role relationships in this chapter must be confined to single-role relationships for several reasons. A major reason is that single-role relationships are the easiest to write about; we have amassed the largest amount of information about them; they are the easiest to predict. Conversely, multiple-role relationships demand a level of sophistication that some would be unable to achieve. Yet again, some achieve it but only where motivation is high. If close kin are involved in a family business, more finely tuned adjustments are likely. Should they fail to occur, the outcome will be subject to the usual laws of team-role working; and the consequences of failure in that case could be more catastrophic because the stakes are higher.

Single-role relationships involve a model that is necessarily more simple than we would like. The consolation, however, is that what follows does apply to a very large number of working relationships. People express themselves in their usual ways and, therefore, given some knowledge of their collaborators, we can say what the outcome is likely to be.

Below, we have set out a summary of the principal forces at work as they affect relationships between the team roles and the three status levels − boss, peer and subordinate. One important point to be noted is that reciprocal relationships are not necessarily of equal value to both parties. For example, a Co-ordinator may work well for a Shaper boss in that in such a setting the CO may achieve a great deal. On the other hand, Shapers do not look for COs as subordinates and generally prefer more compliant Team Workers. The preferred relationships for each team role are considered along with those that are most susceptible to failure.

Shaper relationships

Shapers present particular problems in working relationships. On the asset side they are achievers. They are more likely to gain promotion and to force themselves to the top than any other team-role grouping. On the debit side, many firms run by Shapers are subject to human crises, to rows on the Board, to persistent problems in industrial relations. Yet for all that, they achieve business success. If too many Shapers are removed, relationships improve but the business suffers. One solution, therefore, is to pay more attention to the colleagues with whom Shapers work, to take steps to prevent the consolidation of a Shaper culture and to educate Shapers in the cultivation of multiple-role relationships.

Shapers work most happily for a boss who does not interfere but is there to offer advice if need be. Co-ordinators possess the people skills and the maturity of overview to be able to cope effectively with all but the most difficult Shapers (and sometimes even those!). Monitor Evaluators can make effective bosses of Shapers provided they possess the wisdom to gain respect. With other bosses, difficulties are very apt to occur. Shapers are more prone than other team roles to challenge the establishment. Implementers in particular dislike the disturbance a Shaper underling is liable to pose to a well-ordered system.

In terms of peer-group relations Shapers often appreciate dynamic colleagues with whom a certain amount of cut and thrust is possible. Here Resource Investigators ideally fill the bill. This relationship seems to work to much greater advantage than in the case of the other creative role — Plant. Plants are too protective towards their own ideas: the cut and thrust is seen more as a threat.

With subordinate relations Shapers seem to be best served by Team Workers who are better able than others to deal with Shaper dominance and even to manipulate the boss with discretion. A Completer can also serve a Shaper well, yet there is always the prospect that the tensions may become too great. Implementers generally make good subordinates of Shapers, provided the former are not attached to any remnants of a previous regime. A less satisfactory subordinate for a Shaper is a Co-ordinator. The reason is one of style clash, especially if the relationship becomes too close. The Co-ordinator can often make the most in people-handling terms of the Shaper's drive and desire for results. Yet, paradoxically, what is set in motion may be seen by the Shaper boss as being too slow and indirect. Shapers are inclined to treat Monitor Evaluators in the same way. The risk, however, of a style clash is lower. The problem is that Monitor Evaluators are easily overriden, their advice is not listened to and they may end up with having no real role at all.

Plant relationships

True Plants have a way of being squeezed out of organizations. They do not easily fit into a system unless they disguise their very nature, in which case their potential is liable to be lost. A Plant needs to be orchestrated by another — to have a backer or a champion. The ideal boss is a Co-ordinator. Co-ordinators are good at discovering human talent and knowing where and when to use it. A Team Worker boss, sympathetic and supportive, can also bring the best out of a Plant. At the other end of the scale, Shapers and Implementers are likely as bosses to show the greatest intolerance towards Plants. Since in reality these are the people most likely to run organizations, Plants tend to disappear before reaching senior levels in management. If they reappear, they do so as Consultants.

Plants make stimulating colleagues and associate well with Co-ordinators, Resource Investigators and Team Workers, in other words with those in the social roles. It is another matter with those in the thinking roles. Clashes on theoretical matters are apt to occur with Monitor Evaluators and other Plants, even though they are drawn towards each other. Such debates might lead to valuable outcomes. But general experience suggests they do not unless there is someone in the group who is in charge. Plants most risk clashing with Implementers as colleagues. Their basic aims and values have little in common, while their methods of working conflict. If they associate without any structure, these intrinsic problems are unlikely to be resolved.

If Plants relate poorly to Implementers as colleagues, it is another matter when it comes to subordinates. Whatever differences in outlook occur, the Plant boss/Implementer relationship is one of the most effective if it can be established. If an idea is judged to be practical the Implementer gets on with it. The Plant, too, will sense that airy-fairy ideas will not be acted on. Another valued relationship is with the Monitor Evaluator as subordinate. Here the status difference serves a useful function. As colleagues they would argue. But under this realignment in hierarchy, the Plant is more confident in declaring: 'Let me try this one out on you.' The ME acts as a catalyst. That can help both in the development of ideas and in the taking of decisions.

Plants seem to be least happy with Shapers and Resource Investigators as subordinates. Both are inclined to jostle a Plant out of a preferred line of thinking and problem-solving; to become overbold when the sensitivities of the Plant need to be respected.

Specialist relationships

Specialists take a pride in their work and in the self-regulation of their working activities. Perhaps there is a grain of truth in the allegation that they can do without bosses, colleagues or subordinates. In reality, they will have to deal with them since 'no man is an island'. Here a key factor is the scope that Specialists are offered by their boss. Specialists need bosses who believe in and value their professionalism. This is how Implementers tend to behave as part of their respect for structure. Specialists also favour bosses who give them a loose rein from a belief in the delegation of responsibility. Hence they respond well to Team Workers and Co-ordinators. The opposite situation applies to Resource Investigators and Shapers. Both are disinclined to accept the field of the Specialist as a self-governing territory. They will intrude. But because the intrusion is seldom seen as help, the fruits of this relationship are frequently negative.

In terms of working relationships with colleagues, Specialists appear to work best with Implementers and Team Workers, for whom mutual respect can most easily be built up. It is a different matter when it comes to Plants. Plants see every problem as a challenge and it matters little if that problem resides in the territory of the Specialist. Conflicts can soon develop between ideas and experience. In peer-group relationships, conflicts of this nature are not easily resolved.

In dealing with subordinates Specialists prefer those who treat professionals with respect and who observe standards as they are laid down. Implementers and Team Workers, the same duo who relate well with Specialists as colleagues, also serve them well as subordinates. And, once again, Plants pose a problem but in this case even more so, because Plants prefer lateral thinking to observance of established standards their conduct is liable to be interpreted by a specialist boss as a form of insubordination.

Monitor Evaluator relationships

One major consideration, underlining all others, is that Monitor Evaluators are generally low-profile. They need to be discovered if they are to contribute as fully as they are able and they need support from action people at all levels. Pure ME teams were among the least successful in the Management Exercises we conducted over the years. For these it was a case of 'paralysis by analysis'. MEs need to be kept at a distance from other MEs whether in terms of boss, peer or subordinate relationships.

In terms of reporting relationships, MEs work best for a Co-ordinator boss, who consults and seeks advice, and worst for a Shaper boss, especially the bold and decisive type for whom actions speak louder than words.

For colleagues, MEs need to choose Co-ordinators and Implementers with a facility for liaising well and seeing the practical consequences that spring from decisions. They work least well with Completers and other MEs with whom lengthy debate on small issues often spells delay and uncertainty.

For subordinates MEs are served best by Implementers, especially where the latter are efficient both in devising methods and procedures and in supervising their operation. MEs do not usually clash with subordinates. They need to avoid as subordinates other MEs and, to a lesser extent, Plants, largely because excessive deliberation can spell inaction.

Completer relationships

The aptitude of Completers for following through makes them invaluable as subordinates of bosses who are keen initiators and who value results. Completers work well for Resource Investigators, Plants and Shapers. They perform least well when they report to other Completers, for that type of relationship can create undue tension.

As colleagues, Completers are respected most by Implementers, who tend to share aspects of their style and values. The strongest clash is with Resource Investigators, who are most inclined to see them as fussy and restricted, while they in turn see RIs as careless and erratic.

Completers appreciate reliable and well-organized Implementers as subordinates. They are least well disposed towards RIs for the reasons given above. But these reasons are accentuated when RIs are to be found in a subordinate role.

Implementer relationships

Since Implementers have as their distinguishing mark an exceptional readiness to address the practical demands of situations, systems and organizations, they work well with a broad cross-section of people both as bosses and colleagues. But where relationships do go wrong they can go badly wrong.

Implementers prefer bosses with definite ideas on what they require. They perform especially well when they report to Shapers and Plants who look for good organizing skills. IMPs also favour the Completer boss who values efficient follow-through. Relationships are, however, generally less successful where IMPs become bosses of IMPs. That appears to be a formula for that over-elaboration of organization commonly called bureaucracy.

Implementers work well with Co-ordinators, Monitor Evaluators, Resource Investigators, Completers and Specialists. However, not all relationships at peer-group level work out well. IMPs are prone to engage in boundary disputes with other IMPs and to clash with Plants. In this latter case, differences in orientation, priorities and values can create tensions and even havoc unless there is some mechanism for resolving disputes. Unfortunately, in peer-group relations this is seldom possible without referring matters to a third party.

Implementers are inclined to conduct formal relationships with subordinates. Compliant Team Workers often suit them best. The most difficult subordinates are Plants and Resource Investigators, the team roles least inclined to show respect for established systems and authority.

Resource Investigator relationships

Resource Investigators, being sociable and generally tolerant, are not too fussy about those with whom they work. Where problems do occur, they are more likely to arise by being blundered into innocently than through set-piece clashes.

RIs cope well with Shaper bosses, standing up well to the pressures and yet succeeding in holding their own. They do, however, dislike working for bosses who value precision and keep their subordinates on a short rein. Completers and Specialists are to be avoided in this context.

Completers and Specialists are not to be recommended either as colleagues. Here the problem is largely one of irreconcilable differences in style and the lack of likelihood of any complementary accommodation. RIs are likely to work much better with Implementers and Team Workers, establishing a basis for co-operation without any one party becoming overbearing towards the other.

For relationships with subordinates, RIs gain most benefit from choosing Completers who naturally compensate RIs for all those weaknesses that result from typical RI behaviour, i.e. dashing from one thing to another and leaving a trail of unfinished work behind. In this respect, Completers do not need to be supervised. The required action will naturally take place. RIs are happy to work with a great range of subordinates but these relationships may not always be effective. The danger is that subordinates may spend an undue amount of time waiting with little to do. RIs will not have found time to give them instruction.

Though it may help for RIs to have self-starting subordinates, the most self-starting of these could be Shapers, but Shapers do not serve RIs well as subordinates. The problem here is that the tolerance of RIs is prone to give Shapers too much encouragement in challenging the boss. So the Shaper becomes not a subordinate but, in effect, a competitor. A very unstable relationship will then develop.

Co-ordinator relationships

Co-ordinators are usually adept in handling personal relationships, being able both to give orders and to receive them, and they deal especially well with talented people. But because they have a natural disposition towards management, style clashes can arise, particularly with Shapers.

In fact COs are among the most effective in managing Shaper bosses, including those who are the toughest and the most hard-driving. They will put a given brief into operation but will also stand up to Shapers when necessary. So also, COs make their mark in dealing with Plant bosses, including Superplants. The subtle issues that arise in getting the best out of a Plant's vision yet managing those things that a Plant does less well all come within a CO's capacity for handling relationships in a mature way. COs are less keen on working for a Team Worker boss where the sense of direction may be less evident and where a boss may be sensitive to any usurping of authority.

In peer-group relationships Co-ordinators seldom work well with Shapers. Differences in style and emphasis readily develop and the parity in status relationship means that neither party is likely to give way. COs work much better with the other team roles, but especially well with Team Workers on the social front, and with Implementers on the organization front. Here the work naturally divides between COs handling the people side of the business and Implementers handling the task and methods aspects.

Co-ordinators tend to make good supervisors of subordinates but their talents are especially marked in managing Plants. The distinguishing feature here is that creative and clever people are often very difficult to manage. This is an area where the skills of COs surpass those of the other team roles. If, therefore, a Co-ordinator is intent on notching up a mark on the achievement stakes, there is much to be said for seeking out a talented Plant subordinate. On the other hand, a Shaper subordinate is not to be recommended unless the SH has a secondary PL or RI team role. A strong Shaper subordinate is likely to challenge the style, and probably the decisions, of the CO boss without making the sort of contribution that improves the quality of any ultimate decision.

Team Worker relationships

Team Workers are among the easiest of people to work with. Any dangers that do arise are more likely to relate to effectiveness than to matters of compatibility.

Ideally, Team Workers should report to a strong Shaper boss and, conversely, should avoid as boss another Team Worker whose decisiveness may be held in question.

While TWs can combine with a wide range of colleagues, they work especially well with other TWs, providing mutual support and extracting the most from the team process. They also act as good colleagues for Plants, helping to develop ideas and facilitating their progress through the social system. In contrast, the presence of Shapers can destabilize these relationships and unsettle TWs. Shapers soon establish an ascendency, but if they do so they cease to be colleagues.

Team Workers as bosses like self-starting subordinates who know what they are about and yet pose no threat to the boss. Here Specialists fill the bill especially well. Again, Shapers are the exception. They are liable to introduce discomfiture. Self-starters they may be but they are not self-stoppers. SHs will put pressure on TWs as bosses. An inversion of the status relationship is either threatened or implied.

We should conclude this chapter by reminding the reader that the material covered above concerns primary relationships. The tendencies noted may be mitigated or even negated where secondary roles are brought into play and this depends on the development of an appropriate personal strategy. We will seek to give this subject due attention in Chapter 8.

Meanwhile, we have to consider what can be done when things go wrong in relationships and what steps can be taken to prevent likely clashes arising.

7 *The management of strained relations*

What happens when people are locked together by force of circumstance in a working association into which not one with any advanced knowledge would have entered freely? Can anything be done to stabilize their relationship?

The situation may be likened to having to bat on a sticky wicket where a different style of strokeplay is required. To continue the analogy from cricket, a century is no longer the target. It is more a question of how to survive in order to score a few runs. In such circumstances the achievement of a modest score can be the mark of a great batsman. So also, the ability to handle difficult individuals to some limited advantage is what distinguishes those who have special skills in people management.

But problems in working relationships need not necessarily be linked to basically difficult people. Like heavy rain on a pitch, the phenomenon is bound to occur from time to time. We must accept that unusual or unwelcome conditions fall within the range of what constitutes normality. The manager must learn how to handle them. There is even a need to recognize problems at their very earliest stage.

In almost every large or medium-sized organization individuals can be found who avoid each other unduly, without any mutual hostility being openly expressed. Such avoidance is seldom admitted by both parties, nor is it generally noticed by others, and it falls to the occasional onlooker to observe that two colleagues who might have been expected to combine are never seen together. Conversely, certain pairs will be found to spend much time in each other's company, even though the ostensible reasons for so close a working association are not obvious.

Avoidance is more comfortable than conflict. Yet both can be symptoms of strain. Whatever its variations, the nature of interpersonal tension at work deserves closer scrutiny.

For practical purposes strains in working relationships can be classified as falling into three groups:

- The first involves a failure to see how a relationship can be established and it is this that leads to avoidance. Two parties recognize consciously or unconsciously that they cannot communicate with each other to good purpose. The usual reason is that the basis of an effective role relationship is lacking or is difficult to envisage.
- The second condition relates to an actual experience of a relationship which has been found unsatisfactory for both parties in spite of trying. If it continues, as often it must, and the conflict is contained, the cost may be paid later in an eventual crisis.
- The third condition refers to a paradoxical factor that is present in relationships: both parties enjoy a measure of success on one plane, but on another plane or in a particular setting their relationship falls apart. The resulting agonies may be so traumatic as to prove terminal for the relationship, unless somehow the situation can be retrieved, which it often can, but only through delicate handling or appropriate intervention.

Each of these different sources of strain will now be considered in turn.

Identifying hidden strengths

It is very difficult to establish a successful relationship with anybody without finding something that can be liked or admired. Yet shortcomings are often the qualities first perceived in a person. Weaknesses then tend to be generalized and prejudice can prevent any later recognition of personal assets.

The only constructive alternative, when difficult relationships are in prospect, is to approach the matter from another angle. Starting with the affirmative is to be recommended, even though construction may be difficult where there is not much sign of the bedrock upon which to build.

One starting strategy, especially applicable when dealing with those who have not yet learned to find and manage their own best team role effectively, is to seek positive leads from what may seem an unwelcome trait. In other words the weakness offers clues to a possible strength which will have to be discovered and developed before a proper relationship can begin.

In Table 3.1 we set out negative features of individuals who could make a valued team role contribution. The rationale is that negatives have their positive side. And while the possible good news cannot be presumed we have to act with a certain amount of faith, if we are to make any progress at all, that the conjectured contribution will eventually surface.

For example, a prospective Monitor Evaluator may appear unduly cynical about everything. That is very likely to occur where decisions have been taken and the ME has not been consulted. Cynicism is scepticism gone sour. But scepticism itself is the allowable weakness of MEs. Hence, there are reasonable grounds for believing that some capacity for analysis and judgement does exist. This belief can be tested by asking the particular party for an opinion on another matter in some neutral area. Often a valued judgement will be given and a positive relationship begins to emerge.

Another example arises in the case of an individual who is seen as a vigorous objector and clearly a person to be avoided if peace is to be enjoyed. Objections and complaints commonly take the form in which they upset people unduly and lead to no favourable outcome. All this may sound very negative. The challenging nature of the objector may, however, suggest the makings of a Shaper. Shapers make courageous change agents, ready to overcome obstacles in pursuit of what is seen as a worthwhile objective. It is often a better tactic, rather than tackling such a person head on, to focus on some obstacle beyond the area of current dispute. In effect, the presumed Shaper's energies will be redirected towards the external problem. If the plan works as hoped, the relationship will have produced one positive outcome. More important still will be the likely gain in mutual role recognition.

In general, where a difficult relationship arises because the other party has no evident team-role strength, the prime need is to discover one and to create a situation where the desired behaviour can manifest itself to advantage.

In other words, the difficult person cannot create the conditions that suit him or her unassisted. But if those conditions are created by a planned change of circumstance or by a change in personal treatment, a new pattern of behaviour may be observed.

The easiest change to bring about in close interpersonal dealings is to clarify one's own role position, which may not have been perceived through lack of interest, or it may even have been misperceived. In either case it may need to be spelled out. 'May I explain where I stand. I am not keen on doing so-and-so but I am very ready to do this.' That statement should be in line with one's natural and most favoured team role.

In several instances I have known such a bald statement to yield a remarkably positive response. The reason seems to be that if A cannot comprehend the behaviour of B, then it is probable that B does not know what to make of A. One of the two has to engage in some new initiative if the relationship is to make any progress. The easiest place to begin is often through an act of self-declaration.

Making a team-role sacrifice

If others are unlikely to change, then you may have to yourself. Such a possibility is not to be entered into lightly since it goes against the principle supported earlier of playing to your strength. Yet that principle often has to be sacrificed in dealing with difficult personalities; for it is a feature of such people that they seldom adapt to others. In such circumstances any progress in improving a relationship depends on the self. One is therefore presented with the problem of how to adapt one's own behaviour.

There are two broad options. Both entail some risk of increasing personal role strain. Changing from a natural team role to a manageable team role is certainly an adjustment many make, almost unconsciously, when circumstances demand it. As soon as a boss enters a room people behave differently. For some, this adjustment takes place without tension even if the boss stays a long time. For others the strain may increase appreciably as the moments roll by.

One senior executive with strong Shaper characteristics once told me that he had never got on well with any boss with whom he had worked. One doubts that his boss felt the same strain since this executive had a good record in gaining promotion. Like many a senior Shaper, he possessed well-developed social skills and knew how to use them. However, his natural preference was for combat and confrontation. These proclivities had to be held in abeyance in some situations, which made others feel more comfortable and him less so.

Moving from a natural role to a manageable secondary role is like changing gear. That shift may make one feel as though the vehicle is not going at the speed for which it was designed. Still, the role will need to be one for which some affinity is felt, which is what makes it manageable. In the short term the shift is unlikely to involve much strain. In fact, the experience of engaging in an occasional role shift may even be exhilarating and generate the feeling of extending one's personal skills. But if this form of behaviour is perpetuated the strain will grow as individuals feel cut off from their natural role and in a sense the true self. Those who are required to operate in their manageable roles, rather than their natural roles, for a prolonged period are inclined to seek other jobs, often to the surprise and dismay of the employer.

To change team role is one way of dealing with a potentially difficult relationship. But the big question is into which team role should one change? Manageable team roles can of course be utilized. But whatever roles are readily available may still fail to fill the bill. The situation may require not another role but one particular role that does not form part of the normal repertoire. By studying the primary team role of the difficult person with whom an individual has to deal, the complementary team role can be specified and the requisite behaviour can be acted out.

There are those who have taken this approach to a fine art. They are called con men. The confidence of others can be gained by playing exactly the part that is desired. Of course, adjustments of this nature do not necessarily imply criminality. There are many law-abiding executives who engage in this behaviour for short periods. They are said to be good politically.

One example of such behaviour relates to the Chairman of a large corporation who was deemed to have Specialist team-role qualities. He was a difficult man to relate to and he spent very little time with people outside his immediate personal entourage. His office was equipped with the very latest in technical gadgetry, a point observed by a very creative visitor who needed to do business with this Chairman. In team-role terms the two were unlikely to strike an accord. But in this instance the visitor decided to ask if the equipment could be demonstrated. To this request our Specialist responded delightedly. The interview lasted far longer than had been planned and the relationship proved a success for both parties. Once the business had been concluded there was no longer a need for the parties to meet. The longer-term strength of the relationship was therefore never tested, which perhaps was just as well.

The general principle is that team-role behaviour can be designed to fit the known team role of a given person and acted out in a skilled fashion. Such behaviour will be construed as insincere by those who observe that one party is not behaving in a normal manner. And should that behaviour continue for a period of any length, role strain will almost certainly set in. The more pronounced the role strain, the greater the danger that some sudden breakdown in behaviour will occur, with perhaps unforeseen consequences.

Designing behaviour to fit a given situation therefore involves certain risks. However, other options are available as we will see in the next chapter.

Managing the paradoxical in working relationships

The qualities of social relationships and working relationships are often unrelated. People who are good friends on a social plane may run into unexpected difficulties as soon as they try to work with one another. I once had occasion to work in the same research organization as two very bright young men who had much in common: both were distinguished champions, one in chess and one in bridge, and both enjoyed the same type of wit and prankish humour. Invariably, they went to lunch together and all was jollity until they had occasion to work alongside each other in a project team. That experience produced a transformation. They now spent all their time refuting each other's arguments and propositions. Meeting the objectives of the project became virtually a secondary consideration. Their clashes at work now had the effect of souring their personal relationship.

Friendships grow out of common interests. Yet common interests have little bearing on working partnerships. Instead, working partnerships demand role relationships, especially those of a complementary nature. Often, the team roles are not those that are desired. Even worse, the team roles may be the converse of what might be recommended for any given status relationship. If a Shaper is answerable to a Team Worker, for example, or a Superplant to an Implementer, trouble may be expected.

An example of the latter occurred in a large multi-national which was headed by a Supershaper (Mr Big). Reporting to him was a Team Worker/Implementer (Mr Nice-Guy) who in turn was the boss of a Plant/Co-ordinator (Mr Brain-Wave). All three were highly intelligent men. Mr Big thought the world of Mr Nice-Guy who always rushed to do his boss's bidding. Mr Nice-Guy leaned heavily on Mr Brain-Wave for ideas, being bereft of them himself. Where he considered them appropriate, Mr Nice-Guy passed them on to Mr Big. Suppose Mr Brain-Wave had reported direct to Mr Big or, in other words, a Plant to a Supershaper. That would not have worked and, indeed, the two men were uncomfortable together. So there was something to be said for the existing arrangement with its most uncomfortable associated link – the Plant reporting to the Implementer. This operated in an extraordinary way with Mr Brain-Wave acting as though he was actually in charge of his boss. Mr Nice-Guy would knock on Mr Brain-Wave's door and stand behind the desk of Mr Brain-Wave who with some panache explained what should be done. Later, Mr Nice-Guy would regain his status and establish his seniority in some other minor ways. The element of role reversal and ambiguity in status relationships meant that Messrs Nice-Guy and Brain-Wave were always vying with each other. Yet, in practice, Mr Big derived some real benefit from this unstable arrangement. This became evident as soon as Mr Nice-Guy retired. Then, unfortunately, the whole system fell apart and the attempt to produce an effective linking mechanism in this area of the business failed.

The paradox is that uncomfortable partnerships can produce great results. That is certainly borne out in the case of two of the world's most famous partnerships, Laurel and Hardy in humour, and Gilbert and Sullivan in comic opera. Both pairs experienced great difficulty in working with each other. Stars are happy to work with foils but are disinclined to combine in equal partnerships. In such cases the part played by a third party can be crucial in keeping a pair together. With Laurel and Hardy that third party role was played by Hal Roach, and in the case of Gilbert and Sullivan it was played by D'Oyly Carte.

Since the history of Gilbert and Sullivan is well recorded it is as well to examine how that turbulent relationship survived. The examination should begin with some notes about the players.

Gilbert was by background a civil servant who after being left some money eventually became a barrister but failed to develop a proper practice. His interest in the stage began in an era when musicals were held in disrepute. Sullivan, by contrast, was a professor of music, well known for his compositions and very well connected socially. Sullivan was a ladies man and prone to discreet affairs. Gilbert was loyally attached to Kitty his wife. On political matters the duo also showed contrasting values. The famous refrain — 'Every boy or girl that's born alive is either a little Liberal or a little Conservative' — aptly sums up where the two stood. Gilbert was the former (though in later life his views veered to the right), while Sullivan was the latter.

The evidence suggests that both were Plants. That in itself would pose no insurmountable difficulty due to the functional separation of their areas, with Gilbert's creative powers geared to the plot and the libretto and Sullivan's to the music. It was the additional team roles that caused the problem aggravated by the nature of their status relationship.

Gilbert was not only a Plant but a classic Shaper. He applied continuous pressure on Sullivan and with some justification, since Sullivan was notoriously late in providing the music for their comic operas, preferring to get everything done at the last minute. Gilbert was ambitious in terms of money and in fact made far more from the partnership than Sullivan. But most unfortunate of all, Gilbert even went as far as suing Sullivan during the height of their successful collaboration over the case of a red carpet which, being an extravagance on one of their sets and not previously agreed upon, effectively reduced the profit to which Gilbert felt entitled.

The problem of the relationship between Gilbert and Sullivan was rendered even more complicated by the fact that Sullivan saw himself as the senior person in the partnership. The words were there to support his music and other librettists could be found. Sullivan approached comic opera with some condescension, believing that his talents were better suited to the writing of grand opera, a belief in which he was backed by some of his most eminent admirers. Sullivan's sense of superiority made a working partnership difficult and provoked Gilbert to the extent that he even wrote to Sullivan pleading that the two should work as equals.

Gilbert, the Plant/Shaper clearly had managerial ability but was effectively subordinated to Sullivan the Plant/Specialist during much of their association. The point was emphasized on the social stakes by the award of a knighthood to Sullivan and his reception into the highest circles including the royal family. In terms of team-role theory that combination in such a reporting relationship stands little chance of working.

Yet the relationship did hold together. It needed someone who could see the total picture, who could recognize the synergy that both talented men brought to each venture, who could handle their idiosyncrasies and who had a vision of the future. That person was D'Oyly Carte. Carte was a composer in his own right, yet his energies were directed elsewhere. Carte foresaw the need to make musicals respectable and he attended to all that facilitated this plan, including the introduction for the first time of numbered seats. D'Oyly Carte was the founder of a company so that his name lives to this day. He behaved like a Plant and a Co-ordinator but he was ready to sacrifice his Plant role when the human issues took precedence over business considerations. Carte stopped Sullivan from deserting the partnership due to resentment and his other unfulfilled muscial ambitions. The difficult working relationship held.

Third-party relationships

When two people fail to work smoothly together, it may need a third party, like Hal Roach and D'Oyly Carte, to create and project a sense of working unity.

The converse, however, can also apply. Two people who work well together can be disturbed by the arrival of a third person who is a functional contributor but who complicates, often unknowingly, the essential team-role relationship.

When two people have enjoyed a successful working relationship over a period, they will have learned to assign and take up a complementary set of tasks and duties that broadly correspond with their team-role profiles, though of course it will seldom be expressed in such language. However, the assignment is relative to that relationship. Whoever is the better at dealing with practical matters will take over the Implementer role; whoever has the keenest analytical mind will act as Monitor Evaluator. But that should not imply that one person or the other naturally performs well in that role at a level that would be accepted by a larger group.

The arrival of a third person usually results in a claim to operate in a given role. Let us consider the case of C, who is an accomplished Completer. A is weak in this area and B, while not strong, is certainly a more accomplished Completer than A and so will have taken over duties in this field. The arrival of a true Completer who tidies things up and puts things in order may be resented rather than welcomed. C is seen as fussy and interfering, leaving C disconsolate. What has happened is that B has been valued by A as bringing a missing contribution to the partnership, even if not exactly of a high order, and that contribution is now being undermined.

The tensions that arise when a third person, C, joins a partnership are due to the fact that the nature of the role relationship between A and B is not easily unravelled and is seldom articulated. For C to operate in a natural role is therefore hazardous. To perform well in the role, strange though it might seem to C, would not help either. It would be better to play no role at all for a while until the role that was required could be sensed.

Where the relationship between A and B is on a hierarchical footing, the introduction of C introduces a further complication. C now has to find a place in a hierarchy. Is it as the peer of A or the peer of B? Or is C now the most junior of the three, in which case there are now three tiers in a three-person relationship? Any one of these possibilities will have its own specific bearing on the team-role relationships. And how each one perceives these relationships will need to be brought into line. The likelihood is that some misunderstanding will result.

It should now be clear how complicated it is for any one individual to get on well across the range of working situations involving close relations with one or two people. That is why there is a common preference for sticking with those you know, a preference that extends from the lowest to the highest levels of seniority.

If fruitful progress is to be made in developing personal skills, some risks may need to be taken. And here the creation of a strategy can help. That strategy must be individually tailored since people are so different. Some general guidelines on how to proceed will be put forward in the next chapter.

8 *A strategy for self-management*

Ever since team roles entered the language of industry, executives have favoured for themselves those roles that have the ring of leadership about them. There was a strong attraction to the glamorous sounding title of Chairman, as it was first named following the Henley research. Even when, advisedly, we had to change the term to Co-ordinator, its popularity with the aspiring executive was only slightly diminished. Shaper has even stronger appeal, especially to the ambitious, while others fancy themselves as Plants.

At the other end of the popularity stakes, there are certain roles that have a Cinderella touch about them. Anyone emerging from the team-role analysis with the combination of either a Completer/Implementer or a Specialist/Team Worker often does not feel very flattered, for it sounds hardly the stuff of which top managers are made.

The surprise, which many would scarcely credit, is that the absence of the team roles most generally favoured for the self is a matter of less importance than the skilful management of whatever team roles a person possesses.

This point is well borne out by the exceptions to what is acknowledged as an advantage — that top managers should possess typical leadership team roles. So, occasionally, one hears the following words from someone about to effect an introduction.

> You will be surprised when you meet BB. He is the sort of man you would never notice in a room. Nor in talking to him would you ever guess his position. Yet he founded and built up the company and made a fortune for himself in the process.

Such individuals evidently lack the classic team-role profile of leaders. So how do they do it?

In general, these unexpected successes have one distinguishing feature in common. Notably, they play to their strengths while ensuring that any weaknesses they may possess are never exposed. Any suspect fields in which they might get caught out are invariably passed on to, and well covered by, colleagues.

Arguably this can be a sign of mature sophistication. Or is there a simpler explanation? Can it be that out of modesty, diffidence or a certain shyness, a fortuitous benefit has been derived — freedom from what the ancient Greeks called 'hubris' or the arrogance that springs from power and conceit? Pride comes before a fall, as it frequently does with tycoons, and it was the Greeks who first observed that hubris was the forerunner of a disaster. So our milder-mannered managers and entrepreneurial pioneers enjoy one advantage over their charismatic counterparts — some guarantee of protection from nemesis.

Finding the self

Ancient wisdom has passed on to us the advice that 'to know thyself' helps to keep nemesis at bay. In modern industry it is as though this advice has been heeded. Many human resource training and development establishments make a point of asking their participants to complete psychometric tests and personal inventories with a view to extending their self-insight. By exchanging information on what the tests and inventories say, members of a group learn more about one another. They also come to see the value of taking account of individual differences in the discharge of group responsibilities.

These tests and inventories rely essentially on self-reporting. Most participants respond favourably to the outputs they receive, declaring them to be 'true', a comment that can scarcely be surprising since it is their own inputs that have been processed and fed back to them.

Knowledge of the self is at risk, then, of becoming a closed system into which the perceptions of the external world fail to break. Yet the practice of industry means that when decisions have to be reached about people, in terms of promotion or transfer to other work or, indeed, on any matter of importance, it is the perception of others about the self that forms the basis of decision-making. Such percep- tions are facilitated through annual assessments. Yet here, perception rather than perceptions might be the better word. In what has now become a standard procedure in many organizations it is a single person — the boss — who makes the assessment. Whatever personal relationship exists with the subordinate will colour what is written. Yet, often, the problem lies with the converse: the feedback contains no colour at all. For bosses are in a dilemma. To criticize may be to demotivate. After all, if someone lacks a particular aptitude, not a great deal will be gained by pointing it out. Equally, to be lavish in praise about any personal feature or talent entails risks of another sort. Expectations of advancement will be raised and the organization receives documented information that may be used in a career plan. This increases the likelihood that the immediate boss might lose a valued employee through promotion in an internal move. Faced with this dilemma the usual compromise response is to produce a bland report which leaves the employee craving for something more definite.

In practice, most individuals do not receive much accurate information about the self. Yet the search goes on continuously and usually unavailingly. If the self cannot be found, perhaps it is better lost. In place of the real self, with its potential for specific development, role models are cast before us.

One much favoured way of teaching management is to study outstanding managers and leaders, enumerate their best qualities and hope that by some process, akin to osmosis, these will be absorbed and transferred into the vital systems of the diligent student. Reading biographies of Ghandi or Napoleon or Churchill or Thatcher may inspire one to better things, or not as the case may be. But, speaking personally, I have never observed anyone to change their behaviour to become more effective as a result of such reading. Individuals do not make good carbon copies of one another but only pale shadows whenever they attempt to imitate.

There is, however, a strategy for finding the real self. That strategy rests on reconciling two separate strands of information. One derives from self-assessment and the other from the assessment of others.

At this point we have to accept that the source of that information may vary as people find themselves in different settings, often having to cope with unfamiliar demands. Then behaviour may change from what they would consider normal, so that they surprise, and even try to surprise, themselves. That is why middle-aged managers are to be found on courses in the mountains, seeking to defy all the hazards and inclement weather in quest of a particular goal in group endeavours. Only when a wide range of experiences has been offered and reactions to those experiences assessed can a stable view be formed of what the self can and cannot do and how the self compares with others.

Information derived from the perception of the self and of others about the self needs to be put together systematically, sifted, normalized and eventually integrated to provide a working profile that can act as a reference base for decision-making. The intricate nature of that task may be optimally facilitated with computer assistance. The elaboration of that process manifested itself in what was to become the Interplace System of Human Resource Management.

For the outputs of Interplace to offer a full range of reports, four valid assessors were needed. Computer experts tell us that 'garbage in means garbage out', so the assessors themselves had to be assessed, which of course the computer did for us. In the event, more than four assessors were often needed, since some would be rejected before an adequate threshold was reached for actuating the system.

The final output allowed each participant to match their main contribution to a team, in their own eyes, against what others saw. Three distinct pictures then emerged.

- *The coherent profile.* Here the individual's self-perception lines up with the perceptions of others. Understanding is made that much easier through developing the right sort of mutual expectations. The only risk here is that a person becomes typed and fails to develop enough team-role versatility to meet all situations.
- *The discordant profile.* Others take a common view of an individual which conflicts with the individual's own self-perception. The implication here is either that the self is subject to an illusion which needs to be corrected or that there has been a failure in self-projection. In either case the person with a discordant profile is likely to benefit from counselling since there is clearly an identity projection problem to be overcome.
- *The confused profile.* This condition arises where there is no consistency between the assessors nor any affinity with self-perception. This condition signifies that the self has not succeeded in registering any particular team role and will need to make some decisions if an effective team role is to be developed. Here the counsellor can perform a facilitating function in pointing to any paths that look feasible.

Most people have profiles that lie somewhere between these more extreme categories. Whatever the nature of the profile and irrespective of how it is built up, the lessons for the self are broadly the same. The need is to focus on the lead or natural team roles and to play these to competitive advantage. Here a certain amount of discretion is possible. A team role for which an individual has some aptitude may be deliberately cultivated and in some situations this makes a great deal of sense. For example, on one occasion an accountant who was promoted to general manager, noting that his first team role was Completer and his second role Co-ordinator, decided to drop his Completer image and develop his Co-ordinator qualities. This he did quite successfully, for there were no barriers to development in this direction once the decision was made.

Natural team roles need to be developed further if they are to become conspicuous strengths. For example, it makes good sense for a Co-ordinator/Resource Investigator to attend a communications course but much less sense for a Completer/Implementer to be given the same training. If a person is to make an impact it will be through acting out lead team roles in the most effective fashion.

People who are judged successes in their team roles project them well. They do this through the words and phrases by which they are known. In Table 8.1 we have set out some favourite phrases, including some humorous ones, beloved by individuals strong in particular team roles.

The spoken phrase is not the only way of putting across a point. Occasionally, one sees behind a top executive's desk a framed tableau which expresses a message to all who enter the room. That tableau will attract far more attention than, say, the conventional landscapes that commonly adorn office walls.

Years ago I was struck by a tableau in the office of an aspiring young executive in a large organization. The words simply said PLAN AHEAD. Rather, that is how it should have appeared, for the lettering was so badly planned that the last two letters had to be squeezed in on a slope and in smaller size. Since the company in which this office was housed was prone to headstrong and ill-considered decisions, the statement in the tableau announced a competing style of management. The mark which our young executive made in this way helped to establish his rising, and eventually very successful, career.

Developing a natural style

We can now sum up what is needed to develop an executive style of working attuned to the capacity of the self.

The first step is to discover the self, not merely by introspection but by how the self appears to others, with special regard to what behaviour is and is not appreciated.

For those with a confused or discordant profile this usually generates a certain amount of agony tinged with a compulsive fascination.

The value of the outcome depends on whether the contradictions or anomalies can be sorted out, so leading to a point of arrival. The arrival involves personal decision. In effect, a person needs to say: 'Bearing in mind the information about me, this is how I am going to play things in the future'.

Decision, then, helps to determine style. But that raises a question. If a style is fashioned by information and decision, is it fair to call it natural?

I would maintain that it is fair. Even natural styles involve an element of learning. It is very rare to find that star performers continue a style they started with — a style that naturally happened with no further explanation. A polished performance is usually the end result of a process. The star performer first displays aptitude. That in itself creates opportunity. Opportunity combined with a high level of aspiration produces an awareness of a shortfall in achievement. The gap perceived between what a person can do and wishes to do can now only be lessened by learning. That learning may involve painstaking effort but once it has been completed and consolidated in practice, the style that comes about will lose its erratic features. There will be a certain consistency and coherence about it. Viewed from the outside it will appear a natural style.

Take the case of typing, golf or skiing. It is inconceivable that high performers in any of these arts will have begun naturally and have continued in the style in which they started.

The roots of the current keyboard stretch back deep into the last century and it was fully 40 years before typing with two fingers was replaced by a method which uses all fingers and is now standard. A natural typist will have acquired this artificial method and assimilated it to the extent that it is now natural to the person. So also with golf, few beginners can be expected to move the ball up in the air and in a straight direction. Even golfers who win championships are known to go back to experts to help them reconstruct their swing. Yet they will still be judged natural golfers with commentators quick to point out differences in their individual styles. In the case of skiing, the natural reaction of the beginner peering down a steep slope is to lean towards the rear foot. That action guarantees falling down on one's bottom. Becoming a natural skier involves overcoming nature. Natural reactions have to be suppressed and new ones learned.

Learning a psychomotor skill is not fully comparable with learning managerial behaviour because the former embodies many standard correct ways of doing things. True, there are some correct procedures that all managers would do well to follow. But the standard procedures

Table 8.1   Phrases and slogans that project leading team roles

Plant
1   When a problem is baffling, think laterally.
2   Where there's a problem, there's a solution.
3   The greater the problem, the greater the challenge.
4   Do not disturb, genius at work.
5   Good ideas always sound strange at first.
6   Ideas start with dreaming.
7   Without continuous innovation, there is no survival.

Resource investigator
1   We could make a fortune out of that.
2   Ideas should be stolen with pride.
3   Never reinvent the wheel.
4   Opportunities arise from other people's mistakes.
5   Surely we can exploit that?
6   You can always telephone to find out.
7   Time spent in reconnaissance is seldom wasted.

Co-ordinator
1   Let's keep the main objective in sight.
2   Has anyone else got anything to add to this?
3   We like to reach a consensus before we move forward.
4   Never assume that silence means approval.
5   I think we should give someone else a chance.
6   Good delegation is an art.
7   Management is the art of getting other people to do all the work.

Shaper
1   Just do it!
2   Say 'no', then negotiate.
3   If you say 'yes I will do it', I expect it to be done.
4   I'm not satisfied we are achieving all we can.
5   I may be blunt, but at least I'm to the point.
6   I'll get things moving.
7   When the going gets tough, the tough get going.

Monitor evaluator
1   I'll think it over and give you a firm decision tomorrow.
2   Have we exhausted all the options?
3   If it does not stand up to logic, it's not worth doing!
4   Better to make the right decision slowly than the wrong one quickly.
5   This looks like the best option on balance.
6   Let's weigh up the alternatives.
7   Decisions should not be based purely on enthusiasm.

Table 8.1 (*continued*)

Teamworker
1 Courtesy costs nothing.
2 I was very interested in your point of view.
3 If it's all right with you, it's all right with me.
4 Everybody has a good side worth appealing to.
5 If people listened to themselves more, they would talk less.
6 You can always sense a good atmosphere at work.
7 I try to be versatile.

Implementer
1 If it can be done, we will do it.
2 An ounce of action is worth a pound of theory.
3 Hard work never killed anybody.
4 If it's difficult, we do it immediately. If it's impossible it takes a little longer.
5 To err is human, to forgive is not company policy.
6 Let's get down to the task in hand.
7 The company has my full support.

Completer finisher
1 This is something that demands our undivided attention.
2 The small print is always worth reading.
3 'If anything can go wrong it will', and as O'Toole said on Murphy's law, 'Murphy was an optimist'.
4 There is no excuse for not being perfect.
5 Perfection is only just good enough.
6 A stitch in time saves nine.
7 Has it been checked?

Specialist
1 In this job you never stop learning.
2 Choose a job you love, and you'll never have to work a day in your life.
3 True professionalism is its own reward.
4 My subject is fascinating to me.
5 The more you know, the more you find to discover.
6 It is better to know a lot about something, than a little about everything.
7 A committee is twelve people doing the work of one.

---

are fewer and the scope for individual differences is greater. Nevertheless, in the last analysis, the skill in both fields has to be fashioned round the person until eventually it becomes part of the person. The natural way may need to be modified. But if too much modification is required, the hoped for result is likely to prove beyond reach.

Making a sacrifice

By the time a person reaches the years of discretion, as may be understood in the discharge of executive responsibility, natural styles will either have evolved or they will fail to have evolved. But that does not mean that styles that are not part of the normal repertoire cannot be employed. Indeed, a given situation can often come about where normal behaviour would be unwelcome or could even prove disastrous. In everyday language it is often termed 'speaking out of turn'.

One way out would be to keep silent. But in the case of a manager, more is expected. Managers are supposed to be dynamic and proactive and to contribute something, at the very least. That is the setting in which the need arises for a shift in team roles. A team role can be taken on which is not a natural role but is at least manageable and can be performed with competence. It is fashioned by an awareness of need. However, the role that is adopted will not be performed easily or without a conscious sense of self-discipline.

Take the case of a thrusting Shaper who is required to chair a meeting of high-level executives drawn from other organizations. These executives will not acquiesce on orders or decisions taken from the chair. They expect to be consulted and for the Chairperson to serve the group. The Shaper will need to act in a style that would be natural for a Co-ordinator. But that team role, on the best available data, comes fourth among the nine ranked team roles. What this means is that the Shaper will need to resist behaving in the preferred way and for a limited period of time should opt for behaviour embodying a team-role sacrifice.

The skilful and versatile executive will be able to make the necessary shift. But it would be a mistake to imagine that this acquired behaviour will have much permanence attached to it. Eventually, people revert to type, especially when tiring, irritated or under pressure. The good work can then be undone in a few minutes. An apparently level-headed person will suddenly start a commotion by baiting one of the participants. Or a well-conducted meeting can be terminated with a summary that unduly reflects the particular view taken from the Chair.

Secondary team roles can be performed with distinction for a limited time or discharged adequately for a longer time. But they can seldom be enacted indefinitely and to a satisfactory standard without mishap.

There are, however, a few situations where the pressures are so intense that behaviour in the job remains exemplary. One finds this with deputy managers, who are ideally cast to take on the Number One role but who instead act with the restraint sensed by those who feel their turn will come. The cost of such continuing restraint is personal stress. It manifests itself in psychosomatic illness, nervous breakdown or, more usually, in the sudden and unexpected letter of resignation.

Manageable roles can be worked on with a view to improving personal versatility. Yet if too much emphasis is placed on achieving versatility, it will be a sign that strong natural roles are in danger of being set aside and the individual may end up being miscast.

Contracting out

The art of self-management lies in knowing what to do and what not to do. The not doing is the most neglected part of the art. Yet its importance should be emphasized. Through not doing, time and scope are made available for the doing. The not doing defines the territorial borders of the doing and enables the doing to take on larger-than-life forms.

If we consider the art in terms of separate modules, contracting out can be handled in three basic ways.

One way is to build a team where there is no pressure for the self to make a team-role sacrifice. In a perfectly balanced team there is always someone who can deal naturally with any set of responsibilities. In these circumstances, people do not think consciously about what to do. Things happen with the minimum of verbal communication. It is as though everyone knew in advance the collective intentions of the group and each one slots into place. Life in these circumstances feels easy. The difficult and demanding bit is knowing how to build such a team in the first place. But it is well worth attempting. Building a balanced team, comprising members with complementary qualities, offers the surest guarantee that the self will not need to act out of role.

My experience with balanced teams is not only that they have a certain robustness which enables them to cope with a great range of situations but that they also build up a remarkable resistance to interference.

There have been occasions when I have formed teams for the purpose of a management education exercise and have then offered to avail myself as a human resource consultant to enable the teams that have been constructed on various models to make the best possible use of their members. Unbalanced teams have usually been pleased to see me. It has been an entirely different matter with balanced teams. It has been made plain in no uncertain terms that my presence would be unwelcome.

The balanced team is self-contained, and knows it. It operates as though on auto-pilot, requiring no guidance from the control tower. Should a team feel it needs help, it is a pretty sure indicator that there is something wrong with the balance of the team.

In a sense, life is easy when a team is balanced. But when the balance is not there, other means have to be found for devolving responsibility on those who are suitable to carry it.

That brings one to the second method, available to the self, for avoiding being pushed into unsuitable roles. The method is to focus on the core activity and delegate responsibility for it to someone who is suitable to carry it.

'Delegation' has become so favoured a word in management circles that its mere utterance creates general approval. That carries the danger of masking its real meaning in a team-role sense.

Delegation does not refer here merely to an off-loading in the volume of work and the responsibility attached to it, but to the choice of that responsibility. One does not delegate those things that one is good at doing. One delegates in a field where one's strength is lacking. By contracting out of certain team roles, the self contracts out those team roles to others. The delegation is essentially one of assigning responsibility for a class of work for which a particular team role is central. This still enables a face-to-face and interactive relationship to be retained with the person who now takes on that responsibility.

So, for example, I have overheard in meetings the comments: 'Derek, you're supposed to be the ME (Monitor Evaluator). We've had several ideas put on the table. Which in your opinion looks the better bet for us?'

The person who asks that question relinquishes, by implication, any claim on the ME role and transfers that role to another. The other has not merely been asked a single question on a simple issue but has been given, again by implication, a wider recognition. Derek's role will now be apparent both in his own eyes and in the eyes of the group.

There is, finally, a third strategy that enables the self to avoid unsuitable team roles. It is a strategy rarely used and seldom chanced upon by accident. Yet it is one that is remarkably effective and by no means as damaging to the self as may appear at first sight.

The method bears the title 'Creating A Team-Role Void'. What it means is that the self renounces a team role, implying that a void exists and there is no-one there to fill it, and certainly not the self.

I once heard an account of a dyslexic top executive of a large organization in which paperwork played an important part; yet he had succeeded in establishing his position well before dyslexia was ever talked about or even admitted. This executive, however, valued high personal talent and surrounded himself with clever people. While it is common for a boss to try to outsmart his subordinates and imply mental superiority, our executive took the opposite course. He would say: 'You may be clever guys but these reports mean nothing much to me. I doubt that anyone else will understand them. If you have anything worth saying condense it into not more than a page and a half. And put it in simple English so that even I can understand it.'

This tactic proved a huge success. His associates felt fulfilled and thought the world of their boss. In effect, the boss was renouncing the Plant/Monitor Evaluator role and by this means providing a defined area of opportunity for others.

Declaring a team-role void has special application where the self associates with others whose team roles are unknown so that delegation is scarcely a feasible option. By announcing what is lacking, an invitation is extended to all and sundry to step into vacant shoes. No assumptions are made about the suitability of others who may be present and no-one is ruled out. Competition develops to occupy the space indicated. After some prompting, questioning, discussion and discrimination a suitable candidate can often be found. The gap in the team is plugged.

To sum up the message of this chapter as a whole, each executive can be recommended to adopt a basic strategy in self-management along the following lines even if the contents of the measures adopted will vary from case of case:

1 Establish which team-role styles can be deployed to advantage by the self, bearing in mind the observations of others. Set out to perfect these styles so that they can be enacted with skill and professionalism. Develop favourite phrases and sayings which proclaim the self's claim on these roles. Work to ensure that the team roles chosen by the self will be understood and perceived in a favourable light.
2 Decide on those team roles that, while not naturally part of the self, need to be held in reserve, improved with study and brought out on suitable occasions. Treat these as manageable team roles that entail some team-role sacrifice. Do not be

tempted to stay in less-preferred team roles for long unbroken periods, bearing in mind the dangers of role strain and the risk of being criticized for inadequate performance.

3   Outlaw those team roles that are foreign to the self. Do not allow them to be incorporated into habits or form part of the expectations of others. Remember that the avoidance of unsuitable team roles needs to be actively, and even energetically, pursued. Failure to do so means that the self will be poorly placed and in a weak position.

Carefully considered self-management, rather than the possession of a long check list in competencies, is often what distinguishes the executive who outstrips others. Like the player who scores the goals in sport it is a question of providing the right behaviour in the right place at the right time.

9 *The art of building a team*

The term 'team' is imbued with a meaning derived, in the first instance, from games. Each player in a team game has a position and a specific responsibility. The skills of the players are important but the strength of the team depends more especially on how well the players combine. Star players who fail to pass the ball are no longer an asset and may be dropped in favour of those who fit in best. In the high-performance team, each player knows when and where to enter and to exit. Timing is all important. Indispensable for this context is the knowledge the players have of one another.

Against this template, the word 'team' seems to be used loosely in industry, often being applied to individuals engaged in a common undertaking where their separate roles are ill-defined or non-existent. 'Team' is often used benignly for a group. One hears managers talk in an avuncular fashion of their 'team' when the members are treated as a flock to be herded by the shepherd and his dog into a sheep-pen. Or, where members are well drilled to behave in a disciplined fashion, they belong not so much to a team as a squad. Or, if group members attend a meeting to receive a common message, they become an audience.

The essence of a team is of players who have a reciprocal part to play and are dynamically engaged with one another. In project management, in starting new ventures or in reaching Board decisions that will determine company policy, teamwork is recognized by those with experience as of vital importance. Yet when people look around to build a team, the reality is that the desired constituents are generally absent.

That well-known item of advice for someone asking directions — 'I wouldn't start from here' — often applies to the building of a team. Few team builders enjoy the luxury of starting from scratch. Possibly some members will be joining *ex officio* as representatives of departments or special interests. There will be people appointed on the basis of their functional roles, because their specialist skills are needed, however unsuitable their team roles. Individuals are present that many would be reluctant to include in a team of their own choosing.

Before we consider the best vantage point from which to start, it is as well to consider why things go wrong. How is it that conventional systems go on yielding such poor results?

Where teamwork fails

People at work meet in a particular context, being selected not because of who they are but because of what they are. At a senior level most collective decisions involve heads of departments. Their positions entitle them to attend and so to express their views. The fact that they may all be Shapers with the drive and determination to get their own decisions accepted may be seen as an impediment to good teamwork. But that recognition does little to alter the situation. The same type of meetings continue to be held and continue to fail. The reason is that in most organizations functional structures take precedence over common sense. And without these structures the organization believes it would collapse. 'We have no option,' I have been repeatedly told. Yet there are perfectly good alternatives for coping with this situation, as we will see later. But first there are other pitfalls of which we need to be aware.

Teamwork is so poor in some hard-driving companies that it cannot escape attention. There is an eventual swing of the pendulum. A new chief executive is appointed. The watchwords now become 'communication' and 'participation'. Group exercises are introduced that cultivate a sense of belonging and togetherness. Company newspapers flourish. The promotion of a corporate culture fosters a new type of conformism. Individuals take care not to offer contributions that are counter-culture. A reluctance to disturb the peace of mind of the ruling team or to announce bad news leads to a mood of acquiescent complacency. Unpleasant business and personnel decisions are avoided. Deteriorating financial results follow. The halcyon days come to an end and the company swings back to a hard-nosed leadership.

These, apparently opposite, cultures have more in common than may strike the observer at first sight. Both lack the dynamism that well-created teams can produce because both are founded on standard paradigms. The one is a Shaper culture; the other is a Team Worker culture. Under both systems considerable time and energy is spent in propagating the culture. Neither stands much prospect of succeeding in the long run. Both models suffer from the genetic faults associated with in-breeding and cloning. As on a single-stand plantation, a virus disease can rapidly spread and wipe out the whole crop. There is no built-in resistance. Only hybrids can withstand the disease and remain fruitful. So it is with companies. Only hybrid cultures offer protection against the possibilities of plague. The basic unit of the hybrid culture is the hybrid team. That should be the starting point for building up effective corporations.

Some intermediate steps

Sudden transformations of companies seldom work in practice any more than they do in the political arena. Somehow the new has to grow out of the old. Like a reptile shedding its skin, it is a gradual rather than a rapid process.

Consider the hierarchy in the Shaper culture to which we alluded above. What are the prospects of using the strength of a team for decision-making when the senior members are all Shapers?

The recommended procedure is for the Chairman of meetings to identify complex and contentious issues and propose referring them to a working party for further consideration. The report of the working party is then presented to the meeting at a later date. This procedure allows the Chairman to compose the working party from members outside the hierarchy. Far greater scope will then be available for team-role considerations and even in a company with a Shaper culture there is every prospect that a balanced team can be formed. If the working party does its work thoroughly and imaginatively, it will not be easy for the meeting of top executives to demolish the report, especially if one or two well-prepared allies have been briefed beforehand.

Even when a firm is convinced it has a particular culture, say a Shaper culture, an audit of its personnel usually reveals a far richer seam of team-role talent than is generally realized. What happens is that those whose team roles are not widely esteemed keep their heads down low. They surface only when the occasion permits it.

In general, working parties, based on principles of the balanced team, can be set up in most organizations that are committed to a different style of leadership without making an issue of it. If the team is to advance its claims, it will be judged on purely empirical grounds.

If it meets its goals it will be approved. So will the ideas that lie behind it. By such steps the culture of an organization gradually evolves and changes.

Before there is real scope in an organization for building better teams, a second intermediate step needs to be taken. Good teams cannot be built unless the appropriate raw material is present. Many companies view their personnel requirements narrowly. As a result they effect a cloning policy in recruitment. It will be said: 'The sort of person who succeeds in this organization is . . . .' A little later one hears about the problems to which the organization is subject. The two statements usually have a causal relationship to each other. But this is seldom apparent to insiders. For example, one commonly hears such statements as: 'We are all very good at getting things moving but not so good at finishing', or 'We have a lot of clever people in this company but they are very bad at communicating with one another'.

These deficiencies are best tackled by altering standard recruitment practices. For every new appointment that comes up one can ask: 'Do we really need someone like that? We are quite good in that area already. Can we not find someone who is more . . . ?' These questions gain in relevance when the parameters for the job slot are no longer taken for granted.

When someone leaves a company and a vacancy is created, an opportunity arises for restructuring the position, involving, perhaps, the enlargement of the job of an existing employee. So it will be said: 'Why don't we let So-and-So take over that part of the job? Where we could do with some extra help is in . . . .' Here the missing element needs to be defined in team-role terms.

Once such a procedure is put into operation, great care needs to be taken in managing the placement issue. The right people are often appointed and then promptly put into the wrong slot. The slot has to be tailored to the individual. Moreover, progress in the new slot will need to be monitored continuously. Organizations need to learn how to handle each of the team roles.

Our experience suggests that firms of management consultants, equipped to use team-role technology, have a better record of success in putting this approach into operation than firms that operate unassisted. Part of the reason may be linked to the political power structure and the way in which decisions that reside in it are distributed through the organization. In the highly formalized firm all manner of constraints prevent people making significant changes to standard procedures. Only the outsider can escape the shackles.

Basic steps in team building

The merits of a team should never be assessed without first considering the purpose of the venture and its terms of reference.

What exactly is it that is worth doing? Questions are the real starting points. This one sounds simple enough. But it is easier to pose than to answer. Vast sums of money can be wasted by starting with the wrong premises. The inquiry into the siting of London's third airport cost over a billion pounds and took an inordinate time. The Commission recommended Foulness, the marshland at the eastern end of Essex. The final site chosen was Stansted. It is said the Commission had been given the wrong terms of reference. The development of Concorde consumed an even greater sum of money. Prestige and the technically conceived ambition to build a passenger aircraft that could fly faster than sound lay at the heart of the venture. Whether it would be commercially attractive to airlines was ignored and no independent feasibility study was commissioned. Once all the airlines in the world had declined to buy Concorde, it was virtually given away to Air France and British Airways.

In starting a new venture, nothing should be presumed. Setting the goal is an art in itself. It is something that Shapers and Co-ordinators are particularly good at. They may take their time but once the goal is set, team building can begin.

To build a well-balanced team demands that there is a reasonable supply of candidates, adequate in number and in diversity of talents and team roles. The manager of the project who is so positioned can feel blessed.

Yet the notion that the first step in a project should be the appointment of a project manager, to manage the team, while seemingly logical is a presumption that is not always well-founded. Many projects and new ventures depend on people with very special skills. Sometimes they do not endear themselves to others as colleagues. Some have idiosyncrasies that make them difficult, even very difficult, to work with. But if the highest standards of professionalism are to be reached, their contribution is indispensable. As things stand, project managers when given a free hand are inclined to prefer the experts with whom they feel comfortable.

Few organizations have stumbled on the alternative way forward. It depends on recognizing that genius is sometimes more critical than management. The one is rare, the other less so. Many a genius lies undiscovered until recognized and fostered by someone whose special skill lies in being able to use human talent to advantage.

A surer formula for success, where projects are exceptionally demanding, is to start with a genius or someone with a pre-eminent talent in the relevant area and then to look for a manager who can relate well to that particular person. In practice the two searches can proceed simultaneously until the pairing is ultimately made. We then have the nucleus of a good team and can ask: What now?

The team now needs to be balanced so that all the relevant team roles, together with any special skills, are well represented. If this can be achieved with only a small group of people, so much the better.

The next step is one of casting. As in the making of a film, it is not enough to assemble good actors and actresses. What is essential is that they are ideal for their parts and here the casting director plays a key role. Casting in industry is in fact more difficult than in film-making since in the latter there is no conflict in priorities. In industry, questions of seniority and functional responsibility intrude into casting.

Take the case of a company contemplating entering a new market through varying the design of one of its proven products. The marketing director will be expected, on conventional grounds, to play a key part in outlining the new design and formulating the strategy. But the marketing director may well be a Shaper/Implementer, whereas the commercial director who reports to the marketing director could be a Resource Investigator/Plant. Who then is going to take the lead? The meeting will need to be handled by whoever is chairing it with insight, tact and firmness. Only then can the key team role play the desired part in the discussion and bring about the decision that holds out greatest hope for the future.

The final step that needs general consideration relates to the style in which the whole operation should be conducted. Those high in the social roles thrive on meetings and they need that environment to bring the best out in them. For others, a meeting is a waste of time and they would rather get down to work on their own or work in a pairing with another. So which style should be adopted? The answer, of course, depends on the people present. No decision should be made on style without first conducting an audit of the team members.

What can happen when there is no team strategy

The recommendations set out above may sound reasonable but are very seldom put into practice. And even if an audit were made, would people consider its implications? A good deal of management education would be required before some of the more radical possibilities were entertained.

For example, on the subject of first steps, to pick a key player first and then choose the manager to fit the player would be an exceptional procedure. The conventional procedure is nearly always preferred but often leads to dire consequences.

Take the case of the Sydney Opera House, often used as the symbol of Australia and perhaps the world's most famous example of modern architecture. This building is a mark of the genius of the Danish architect and winner of the open competition for the design, Joern Utzon (whose design, incidentally, was rescued as an after-thought by the assessors from the waste paper basket). Great credit is also due to the consulting engineers, Ove Arup, who had to overcome many formidable technical problems. That is the sum total of the good news. The bad news was the price paid for mismanagement, thereby stopping the whole operation from becoming a triumph.

The facts were that Joern Utzon was responsible for the design shell but was frustrated in attempting to widen his architectural responsibility for the project as a whole. In due course Utzon was replaced by an architect appointed by the Ministry of Public Works acting for the State Government of New South Wales. In their haste to get things moving, foundations were laid that later had to be dug up and started again since they were not integrated with the requirements of the design. The Opera House itself, from the point of view of capacity and performance, is inferior to what exists elsewhere, even in Australia; there is the barest car-parking facility; and the costs of construction exceeded the original estimate by a factor of ten. The fact that it is a magnificent landmark is all that survived the original conception.

With hindsight, one can see that Utzon belonged to that category of genius who needs orchestrating, defending, supporting and perhaps even mentoring. Precisely who could have worked with Utzon to advantage would have been a critical decision.

The more brilliant the Plant in a team and the more complex the project, the greater is the need to master the arts of project team-building and team-management.

When to keep and when to change the team

It makes good sense, as in sport, to keep a winning team. The members will not only have learned to understand one other but their morale will have been reinforced by success. There is little point in changing a team unless there is good reason for doing so.

While teams should be changed due to poor results, there are also occasions when teams need to be changed in advance of likely failure. Clearly, this is something that is much more difficult to judge. The situation occurs on multi-stage projects where the change in emphasis has strong team-role implications. Research and development preceding the design and launch of a new product typifies the problems that can arise in a multi-stage project. Here there are six critical stages, each of which has to be successfully accomplished if the heavy investment involved in R & D is to yield a proper return.

The six stages in question are as follows:

1 *Identifying needs.* Some projects fail because the wrong targets are set. Key figures at this stage are individuals with a strong goal awareness. Shapers and Co-ordinators make their mark strongly in this area.
2 *Finding ideas.* It is often easier to formulate an objective than to decide how that objective can be achieved. Nothing begins to happen until someone has some ideas on how to proceed. Here Plants and Resource Investigators have a crucial role to play.
3 *Formulating plans.* Thinking about how it is all going to happen involves two prime activities. One entails setting out and weighing up the options, so providing pointers to the right decision. The second demands making good use of all relevant experience and knowledge so that any plans developed have the stamp of professionalism upon them. Monitor Evaluators make especially good long-term planners and Specialists also have a key role to play at this stage.
4 *Making contacts.* No plan is ever accepted unless people are persuaded that an improvement is in prospect. Ideas and plans need to be championed by cheer leaders who can drive home their value and win over the doubting Thomases. This is an activity in which Resource Investigators are in their element. But whipping up enthusiasm is not enough. Each new practice conflicts with an old one. Some disturbed group will need to be appeased. The best appeasers are Team Workers.
5 *Establishing the organization.* One can never be sure that anything is going to happen until plans are turned into procedures, methods and working practices so that they may become routines. Here Implementers are in their element. These routines, however, need people to make them work.

Getting the people to fit the system is what Co-ordinators are good at.

6 *Following through.* Robbie Burns reminds us that 'the best laid plans of mice and men gang aft awry'. Too many assumptions are made that all will work out well in the end. Good follow-through benefits from the attentions of concerned people. This is where Completers make their mark. Implementers, too, pull their weight in this area, for they pride themselves on being efficient in anything they undertake.

Experience shows that, all too easily, key individuals are operating at the wrong stage. For example, a dominant inventer will all too commonly work on detailed plans and organization. He or she will hang on through a sense of ownership of the original idea and a reluctance to let go. Not only will his (her) own contribution be poorer than the situation demands but (s)he may be standing in the way of someone ideal for the job. So, because individuals have performed well at an early stage, there is a natural, though mistaken, assumption that they will perform well at the next. We may easily end up with the right people in the team but all playing the wrong parts. Once again, a casting director is needed if the talents of the team are to be used to best advantage.

Who is to perform the role of the casting director in a company? Whatever the ideal answer might be, the reality is that the role usually belongs to whoever sits in the seat of power. Perhaps that is why the management of human resources is now being increasingly recognized as a top management skill.

And if the skill is not held by the top person, it will need to be exercised by another if the organization is to survive and progress.

The technology of casting

Once material is fed into a computer system it is very easy to retrieve. Under the system known as Interplace III, a person claiming a particular set of team roles through self-description could be assessed against the perceptions of others. If the self-assessment and the observer assessments matched reasonably well, one could be sure that a given individual had the team-role strengths claimed. We would call such a person a good example of the type. It would then require only a short step forward to specify in principle which team-role shapes were required in a team. The best examples of the type would be computer nominated in a few seconds. In that way an ideal team could be conceived on the drawing board, as it were, and the appropriate names would appear so quickly that time would be of virtually no account. Technologically, the means of finding the ideal team in a large firm would have arrived.

Of course, the matter is not as simple as this. There are immense political differences in pulling people out from different parts of an organization to serve in a team. As one problem is solved another is created. How to handle the political process is likely to become the new focus of attention. Good examples of a team-role type are usually in wide demand.

Finding the ideal team by a method not unlike computer dating can also throw up unlikely candidates. These will comprise the 'suitables but ineligibles', the subject we addressed in Chapter 4. Casting directors will be better equipped than ever before to handle this subject and to test out ideas about who will fit in where. They will be seen as taking risks in moving people around. But the risks will be worth while if they lead, as intended, to 'surprise fits'. The surprises will be greatest for those who have thought about people primarily in functional and experiential terms and who, by putting confining job titles on their employees, have restricted the scope of their careers.

For the casting director those computer selected on team roles will be good bets. The price paid is that their backgrounds may not conform to the preconceived ideal. But trials suggest one bedrock on which the future can be built. Newcomers will always be welcome when they can supply qualities and characteristics complementary to other members of the team.

10 *Solo Leader versus Team Leader*

Every enterprise, organization or venture needs a manager to husband resources and deploy them efficiently. But while managers are essential and plentiful, leaders are needed only in special circumstances and are generally in short supply. Their very scarcity causes them to be highly admired and idealized. Their remit is more extensive than that of a manager. Charles Handy, in his illuminating essay on leadership* defines a leader as follows:

> A leader shapes and shares a vision which gives point to the work of others.

On that definition one may deduce something about the team roles that best fit a leader. The word 'shapes' denotes Shaper. 'Vision' conjures up Plant. There is, then, a case for demanding at least one of those team roles for a leader as defined by Handy.

Let us take vision first. Vision implies a uniqueness of insight and overview, a quality ideally supplied by a Plant. If 'vision' comes about instead through a social process, as by consensus, some element of compromise will be likely and the cutting edge of true vision will be lost. A feasible alternative is that vision may be 'borrowed' from another source and then treated as a product of the self. In that case, the borrower, having established ownership of the vision, needs the driving force to project it; and not only that but the allied quality of preparedness for the confrontation involved in defending the vision successfully and seeing off rival visions and goals. A strong Shaper who satisfies those conditions may therefore be counted a leader without being truly imaginative in a personal sense.

Whether there is a difference between business leaders and political

---

* Handy, Charles, 'The Language of Leadership' in *Frontiers of Leadership* (eds Syrett and Hogg), Blackwell, Oxford, 1992.

leaders now warrants attention. There is of course an important difference in the circumstances in which the two can thrive. Successful political leaders need to create a myth about their heroic qualities; they have hardly arrived unless the core of committed supporters believes in the infallibility of the leader. For that reason it helps in the cultivation of the myth when leaders are personally convinced that only they are in possession of the truth. That paranoid feature of those who wield supreme political power is best served by the temperamental qualities characterizing certain types of Shaper. One refers to those who combine anxiety, and even pronounced neuroticism (typically manifested in persecution mania), with an apparent self-confidence. For this special group, myths are self-cultivated for they serve the purpose of enhancing and protecting a vulnerable ego.

For business leaders, myths may play a part in helping to establish their image. But such myths are bound to be short-lived, for business leaders depend ultimately for their survival on the reality of business success. Here the relative claims of Plants and Shapers are more evenly balanced. Far-seeing vision may provide the foundation stone on which long-term success is built; equally, business success may rest on sheer drive and vigour plus the readiness to correct any mistakes made in pursuit of a long-term goal quickly.

On this view about the principal parameters governing leadership, whether in the political or business spheres, it is difficult to envisage how other team roles, especially those such as Team Worker or Implementer, can so readily provide the attributes of a potential leader. While it may be true that all the team roles offer opportunities for reaching top management through the cultivation of an appropriate management style, the same cannot be said about leadership in the way in which we have understood it so far.

For those who argue that certain team roles are debarred from taking on a leadership role, a counter-argument can be voiced on their behalf. It may be asked: Is leadership really necessary or desirable?

The foundation stone of this objection is a re-definition of leadership, with the preference for its more literal meaning being 'a capacity to cause others to follow'. So, an ability to mesmerize a crowd or to win financial support from a body of bankers on slim evidence would constitute leadership. Leadership cannot operate, so it is argued, without followership.

The fruits of this type of leadership, of which followership is an indispensable part, have to be offet against the damage rendered by misleading others or turning them into lesser men and women. Hitler may have been a great leader in that he brought about followership in a civilized country on an unprecedented scale; yet he did not prove a success on any acknowledged criterion of performance.

The question thus arises: Should a failed leader be replaced by another leader or should the whole risky formula of leadership, with its inner mythical core, be abandoned?

Contrasting styles of leadership

The dilemma we face in being attracted to, and being equally repelled by, notions of leadership may be overcome by making a distinction

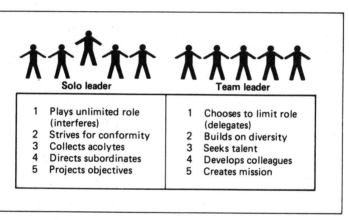

Solo leader	Team leader
1 Plays unlimited role (interferes)	1 Chooses to limit role (delegates)
2 Strives for conformity	2 Builds on diversity
3 Collects acolytes	3 Seeks talent
4 Directs subordinates	4 Develops colleagues
5 Projects objectives	5 Creates mission

1 Plays unlimited role – the Solo Leader interferes in everything.

2 Strives for conformity – the Solo Leader tries to mould people to particular standards.

3 Collects acolytes – the Solo Leader collects admirers and sycophants.

4 Directs subordinates – subordinates take their leads and cues from the Solo Leader.

5 Projects objectives – the Solo Leader makes it plain what everyone is expected to do.

1 Chooses to limit role to preferred team roles – delegates roles to others.

2 Builds on diversity–the Team Leader values differences between people

3 Seeks talent – the Team Leader is not threatened by people with special abilities.

4 Develops colleagues – the Team Leader encourages the growth of personal strengths.

5 Creates mission – the Team Leader projects the vision which others can act on as they see fit.

Figure 10.1 *How do I perform as a team leader?*

between what can now be detected as two diverging styles of leadership in industry.

In the past our concepts and experience of leadership have revolved round the Solo Leader. The leader, familiar to us, is the one with ardent followers who unhesitatingly takes on any role and assumes any responsibility that would otherwise fall into the province of a subordinate. The Solo Leader enjoys free range and rules as if absolutely. This mode of behaviour carries the advantage that departmental barriers and obstacles can be overcome and decisions, urgently needed, can be put into effect without time delays. It is small wonder that in times of crisis talented Solo leaders have come to the fore and have been able to achieve so much.

However, there are other circumstances, in which complexity poses greater problems than urgency, where Solo Leadership is less appropriate. Happily, an alternative is available that should now command our attention. We may refer to it as Team Leadership. The essential difference is that the Team Leader deliberately limits his or her role and declines to rule as if absolutely. That self-limitation will show itself in a number of ways.

First, the Team Leader does not expect to be wiser, more creative or more far-seeing than colleagues, and in consequence is more humble than the Solo leader. For that very reason the Team Leader seeks talent in order to compensate for any personal shortcoming and to improve the balance of the team. The Team Leader is less interested, and often not interested at all, in admirers and sycophants.

Second, by having a greater degree of respect for, and trust in, others the Team Leader is more inclined to delegate, does not interfere with the way in which others operate and is more concerned with outcomes.

Third, the Team Leader fulfils a leadership role by creating a sense of mission. Mission creates the framework whereby each person contributes in their own peculiar way to the common purpose. In that respect the selection and development of the team is crucial. The assignment of responsibility would otherwise be no more than an act of faith.

Very different, then, is the directive approach of the Solo Leader who prefers to dole out tasks and specific goals, who expects compliance, and takes no risks with people. The Leader is the model which others are expected to follow. When, inevitably, Leaders fail, they are discarded.

If the Team Leader does not personally possess vision or the ability to 'shape', in what respect can the Team Leader fairly claim to lead? The answer lies in understanding the nature of leadership and the qualities it requires, in having the humility to appreciate that these may not be strong points in the self, in possessing the people skills to recognize them in others and in the strength of purpose to draw suitably gifted individuals into the team.

That combination of qualities is rare. It occurs naturally in some Co-ordinators but otherwise can be learned. Of course, 'naturals' learn it more readily than others.

One may ask why it is that Team Leadership, rare though it may be, has come increasingly to the fore in recent years.

I think there are two answers. The first is that we are living in a world of increasing uncertainty, characterized by a process of discontinuous change. One person can no longer comprehend everything or provide the direction that can cover all occasions. The second answer is that team leadership is the only form of leadership acceptable in a society where power is shared and so many people are near equals. As dictators fall, whether in the state or in industry, people seek a type of leadership other than one that comes down from high above.

Some consequences of the two leadership styles

Of the two leadership styles, the one familiar to most people is that of the Solo Leader; indeed many are unaware that any other type of leader exists. That is because it is part of crowd psychology to seek to be led and to have faith in the leader.

Sometimes that faith is justified. A leader may possess such a capacity for inspiration, such an ability to sense in what order priorities should be placed and such an ability to win wide support that to follow produces a better overall outcome than to question. When many people feel that way, the leader enjoys unlimited scope. By taking advantage of that opportunity, the leader can accomplish a great deal, whether for better or for worse.

The Solo Leader, however, can only move ahead along a declared path. To retreat, or to engage in even a tactical withdrawal in the event of a setback, would undermine faith in the leader. Errors, therefore, cannot be admitted and in general go undetected (by the leader) and therefore uncorrected. That compounding of errors leads to more serious consequences than the mere commission of management mistakes; it can lead to disaster or something pretty close to it.

I have sometimes talked of this issue as the Napoleon Bonaparte phenomenon. There is no doubt that Napoleon was one of Europe's most brilliant military commanders and political leaders. But that did not stop him committing the gravest errors in his latter days. These have become almost legendary. The painting called 'The Retreat from Moscow' presents this in visual form, while the phrase that 'he met his Waterloo', has entered into everyday usage in the English language. In colloquial English, it means his comeuppance.

The Team Leader has a much less glamorous image. Team Leaders of the purest form hardly exist in politics, since the nature of the political message depends to some degree on the creation of a myth. Without the endowment of the myth, political leaders are scarcely credited with the stature to lead. Even in industry nearly all well-known leaders are marked with the Solo Leader stamp. Fortunately, I have enjoyed the personal opportunity of acquaintance with a few Team Leaders who have held the highest office in organizations that have enjoyed considerable and consistent success. Yet with one exception their names are unknown outside their organizations. Why should that be?

The answer, it would appear, it that while Solo Leaders thrive on, and even crave for, personal publicity, Team Leaders often shun the limelight and avoid taking credit for themselves for whatever successes their organizations have gained. That might be attributable to shyness in some cases. But I do not believe that to be the general explanation. Rather, they recognize that to take personal credit would damage relations within the team and would distort the reality about how that success was actually achieved.

Variations on a theme

The classification of leaders into two groups is of course an oversimple abstraction. Many leaders have a bit of both types in them; or, more generally, they start with hybrid qualities and as success goes to their head they gravitate increasingly towards the style of Solo Leader.

During the course of our work we have learned more about the perception and therefore perhaps the reality of given political leaders than we have about business leaders. The reason for this is that it is easier to build up a database on well-known figures by using assessment techniques than it is to carry out a similar exercise on business figures who mainly operate beyond the public view.

Our two favourite subjects for exercises of this nature were Margaret Thatcher and Ronald Reagan. As erstwhile leaders, they were chosen because both were well known by nearly everyone (and due to their frequent appearances on television, in almost an intimate way). An added advantage was that, while they were friends and broadly took the same political line, their styles of leadership were of a strongly contrasting character. These marked differences served to underline the point that team roles are determined less by the demands of the job than by the character of the person.

The exercise we used was to employ the observer assessment sheets which formed part of our Interplace package. This comprised two lists of adjectives: List A consisted of words used in a favourable sense, while List B embodied a shorter list with less favourable words. The constraints on responding to the items on the list were few. An item could be missed, ticked or double ticked, as the responder thought most appropriate, for there was no forced choice. The meaning in team-role terms would be sorted out by the computer since every word was programmed to have team-role loadings. The exercise was completed by individuals and groups, so giving us a broad picture of the perceived behaviour patterns of the two leaders. The results are shown in Figure 10.2.

Thatcher's natural team role is that of Shaper with one of the strongest scores we have seen in that direction. We found, incidentally, that her overall profile differed very little between those who regarded her highly and those who were ranged against her, the differences lying mainly in whether the favourable or the unfavourable words were used to describe the same team role. Generally, it is clear from analysis of the words ticked that Thatcher is seen as a classic Solo Leader. Whatever her abilities may be, she is not seen as consultative, or diplomatic or interested in others but as hard-driving and aggressive. The team role for which she has least affinity is that of Team Worker.

Reagan, by contrast, is strong on all the social team roles, with his lead role being Resource Investigator. The picture fits happily with the title he has earned as The Great Communicator. His weakest team roles turn out to be the cerebral ones, Plant and Monitor Evaluator. On the score of Plant he has the allowable weaknesses of that role (e.g. forgetful) without having the corresponding strengths.

So what happened in the end? Reagan, in spite of his charismatic qualities, behaved more like a Team Leader during the early part of his Presidency, with some able people operating behind the scenes. As an actor he was content for his scripts to be written for him. On the occasions when he did speak spontaneously, as in answering questions, embarrassment often followed, with a spokesman stepping in with a correction to explain, on behalf of the Administration, what

Assessment results in ranked order

Candidate: Reagan
Observer*
Assessment

Observers

Team roles:	1	2	3	4	5	6	7	8	9
1	RI	TW	CO	ME	IMP	SP	CF	PL	SH
2	RI	SH	TW	SP	CO	IMP	ME	CF	PL
3	RI	SH	TW	CO	SP	CF	ME	IMP	PL
4	TW	IMP	RI	SH	SP	CF	CO	PL	ME
5	CO	PL	RI	TW	ME	SH	SP	CF	IMP
6	RI	CO	SP	TW	PL	IMP	SH	ME	CF
7	SH	RI	SP	CO	CF	IMP	TW	PL	ME
8	RI	CO	TW	ME	CF	IMP	PL	SH	SP

Assessment results in ranked order

Candidate: Thatcher
Observer*
Assessment

Observers

Team roles:	1	2	3	4	5	6	7	8	9
1	SH	CF	SP	IMP	ME	PL	TW	RI	CO
2	SH	CF	ME	SP	IMP	CO	PL	RI	TW
3	SH	RI	SP	PL	ME	IMP	CO	CF	TW
4	SH	SP	PL	CF	IMP	ME	CO	TW	RI
5	SH	SP	RI	CF	CO	ME	IMP	PL	TW
6	SH	SP	RI	IMP	CF	ME	PL	CO	TW
7	SH	RI	ME	PL	IMP	CO	SP	CF	TW
8	SH	RI	SP	ME	CO	CF	IMP	PL	TW

*Observers at management seminar using an assessment technique.

Figure 10.2 *Profiles of two former world leaders. Political co-operation was facilitated by complementary team roles*

the President actually meant to say. However, towards the end of his Presidency Reagan gained a certain confidence in his ability to think things through and to make personal decisions, for it was Reagan who inspired the so called Irangate episode. Unlike Nixon with Watergate, Reagan survived this strategic debacle. When finally he had to give up the Presidency, being no longer eligible for re-election for a third time under the American Constitution, Reagan had lost little of his personal popularity and the American public forgave all. In due course, Vice-President Bush took his place on a wave of continued support for the Reagan Administration.

Thatcher, by contrast, personally spearheaded her long period as Premier of the United Kingdom. Like a classic Solo Leader she replaced all the members of her original cabinet one by one, sometimes after open disagreements and rows. But her attempts to construct a cabinet of those who, in her own phrase, were 'one of us' failed to stabilize her position. Her downfall eventually came about not through the strength of the Opposition or electoral defeat but through rejection on the part of her own team and political associates.

One crucial issue leading to her downfall was the Poll Tax, a standard tax raised on all registered voters irrespective of income. Since some had an insufficient income to be able to pay, there were countless appeals and anomalies and wilful refusals to pay the tax, all of which inflated the costs of handling the whole business enormously. After relentless and largely fruitless attempts to enforce the tax, the political prospects began to look bleak for her Administration. As it transpired, all the problems encountered had been foreseen by some of Thatcher's colleagues. But their advice was not heeded. Nor was Thatcher prepared to backtrack or admit the error of the original decision. The demise of Thatcher after her earlier achievements exemplifies the classic pattern of the Fate that ultimately befalls so many Solo Leaders.

The role of political leaders encompasses all manner of considerations. One objection raised against Dwight Eisenhower, when he was President of the United States, was that he spent a lot of his time playing golf. For a Solo Leader that would constitute a problem, for the implication of negligence would undermine the image. But golf need not be seen as a distraction from urgencies requiring attention; instead it can be regarded as providing the occasion for purposefully developing the style of a Team Leader, which was what Eisenhower was good at. President Jimmy Carter preferred, on the other hand, to keep close day-to-day control, surrounding himself with intimates from his own home State, nicknamed the Georgia Mafia by his opponents.

To some extent, all leaders can make personal decisions about the style in which they wish to operate. They may opt for a style at either end of the Solo Leader-Team Leader range or they may choose something in between. But whatever decision is made or whatever the style adopted unconsciously, the consequences will be far-reaching.

The issues are so important that it is worth considering one principal dilemma that many managers aspiring to become leaders face.

The interface of beliefs and team roles

While it is arguable that all Solo Leaders are Shapers, it does not follow that all Shapers are Solo Leaders. As we saw in Chapter 3, behaviour patterns are a compound of a number of different forces. While it is true that personality may be a predisposing factor, any pattern of role behaviour that would normally be expected as an outgrowth of personality can be overridden by a particular set of values and beliefs. For example, some Shapers have a pronounced attachment to democratic values. They are fully persuaded that social participation and sharing are activities to be encouraged. That poses the question as to what personal style they should adopt when cast in a leadership role.

Situational factors may also call for the modification of a leadership role. Take the case of a manager who has acted like a Solo Leader when in charge of a small outfit and now finds himself heading a large-scale operation. Outcomes there are found to depend on factors that lie well beyond personal knowledge and experience. For example, trading conditions may be affected less by operational efficiency than by movements in currency and changes in raw material prices on world markets. How should the born Shaper with the mental ability to realize the importance of these critical factors now behave?

The answer in both these cases is that while a Shaper may feel more comfortable acting like a Solo Leader, it is inescapable that the naturally preferred mode of leadership is unlikely to yield the desired result. The issue of self-management now becomes a major part of the problem. One possibility is for a Shaper to participate in more consultative meetings. But that option carries the risk that the Shaper may spoil the meeting and make it less productive than it would otherwise be. Occasionally, a Shaper will report to me that his or her staff are having a meeting and have asked that he or she should not attend. In a normal way that would be interpreted as an act of effrontery. But no. Its mention has been associated with pride. The insightful Shaper accepts that there is an autonomous team in operation which is now proceeding well under its own momentum. That pride can be compared with that of a mother who perceives that a child is no longer attached to her apron strings.

A Shaper who believes in the merits of teams and in the sharing of responsibility often faces a dilemma in general terms. Will (s)he barge in like a typical Solo Leader as in days of old? Will (s)he make a team-role sacrifice in personal conduct when associating with colleagues and subordinates? Or will the Shaper declare inwardly: 'This is a situation that I had better keep out of. I know if I enter it I will spoil things. But I am happy about how things are moving in the interests of achieving our long-term goals'.

By adopting the last of these options a Shaper can avoid becoming a Solo Leader and can take the necessary steps to foster team leadership, intervening strongly only when and if the occasion demands it.

Let us consider now the converse circumstance which occurs when a natural Team Worker is presented with a situation which seems to call for a Solo Leader. The Team Worker would prefer to behave like a Team Leader but to do so would create disappointment. People are waiting to follow and therefore want to be led. How should the Team Worker act now?

Here we have to recognize that people seek clarity and decisiveness, often in situations which are fuzzy or where the best option is not all that preferable to the second best. In these circumstances consultation and debate within a small balanced circle of talented people often produce the optimal outcome in terms of the decision reached. The problem now becomes one of presentation. A marginally better decision has to be projected with confidence and charisma. This is not an unduly tall order for an adaptable Team Worker. It merely entails a team-role sacrifice for a limited period of time; it means acting the part and then reverting to the natural self within a circle of close immediate colleagues.

Leadership within a context

Styles of leadership are much influenced by personality and team-role type. But other factors also need to be taken into consideration if a leadership style is to prove right for the situation. The expectation of others and the nature of the culture in which leadership has to be exercised all have a bearing on what line is best taken.

Over the years I have encountered a few large organizations that have given their managers considerable autonomy in terms of how they have run their own particular units. The result has been a diversity of leadership styles with some fairly extreme figures at both ends of a democratic—authoritarian spectrum. Since these units have been independent profit centres, the effectiveness in financial terms of the various styles of leadership can be compared. While this information has not been collected in a way that would satisfy a research study, what has been reported to me on good authority is what we might call a null result; in other words that there are no clear signs that one type of leadership necessarily produces better results than another. It would seem that an able Solo Leader is better than a mediocre Team Leader, and vice versa.

Such reports emanate from units of intermediate size operating in fields of only moderate complexity. It is another story when we deal with the management of large organizations. There, the trend has been to move from Solo Leadership to Team Leadership, usually with beneficial results. Even so, there are still a few brilliant Solo Leaders who buck the trend. Solo Leadership provides more scope for talent but also more opportunity to make ruinous mistakes. This is the trade-off that large organizations have to make when considering which sort of leaders to appoint.

I believe, however, that the future looks brighter for Team Leaders than for Solo Leaders because we now know far more about what constitutes a good management team than we did in the past.

The challenge we have to face in the future is how the flair so often found with Solo Leadership can be retained without losing the all-round strength and reliability of Team Leadership. This item is a new one on the agenda of top management. It is one that will command increasing attention in the years ahead. From what I have seen here and there, I feel confident that the apparent contradiction is less than it seems. The transition from one type of leadership to another falls within the bounds of possibility for many who possess managerial and visionary talent. But it will not happen without a good deal of prompting. And it will certainly be aided by exposure to some carefully planned management education.

11 *The management of succession*

When a person leaves a position to take up another appointment, or retires, or, as occasionally happens, dies while still employed, a search begins immediately for a successor. To find someone with adequate, or perhaps even better, qualifications is relatively easy. The difficulty lies in predicting whether that person, if appointed, will show the desired pattern of behaviour.

But what is the required pattern? At this point the search for a successor divides along two paths. Some will pursue the path that aims at finding a successor who will be worthy of — and resemble as much as possible — the honoured predecessor. Others set off in a different direction, abandoning any attempt at continuity, and seeking instead a successor who will chart a new way forward. In the private sector the challenge may entail the difficult task of refloating an enterprise that has, as it were, run aground; in the political arena, what is needed is someone with a new theme and who perhaps, with a firm hand on the tiller, will stand at the helm to steer the ship of state on some different course.

Decisions about succession embody important choices based on beliefs about both the current situation and the past. How best to act on these beliefs involves more complex considerations than are generally realized.

Let us follow the first of these paths, the most straightforward, where continuity is the order of the day. I have travelled along that road a good many times and this is what I find tends to happen.

Where can we find another Tomkins?

An honoured executive leaves the job and the task falls on someone to find a successor. 'What sort of person do you want?' one asks.

The answer relates not to the demands of the job nor to any analysis of the challenges that lie ahead. 'We need someone like Tomkins. The closer we can get the better', is the reply. An enthusiastic description now follows of what Tomkins was like. One learns in due course that the nature of the job and the boundaries that defined it were very much a matter of what Tomkins caused to come about. The job may have been there all along with the same job title. But Tomkins transformed it. The real content was different. We might even say: 'The job was Tomkins.'

The organizations that begin a search for another Tomkins face an uphill struggle. Unfortunately, Tomkins did not possess a twin brother; or for that matter a twin sister. Any replica of Tomkins that is wheeled in will soon be unmasked as an impostor. 'Not a patch on the real Tomkins.' Those most disappointed with the new appointment will be the most intimate of Tomkins' subordinates and colleagues.

For those acquainted with team-role theory the explanation is obvious. Tomkins' successor will have been chosen from a list of eligible candidates. The likelihood that, from this restricted list, the chosen candidate will share the same team-role profile as Tomkins is remote in the extreme. Why it matters is that the more successful Tomkins is judged to have been in the job, the greater the likelihood that some of the credit is due to colleagues and subordinates who between them made up a good team. The team-role balance is what is critical. The new appointee disturbs the balance. Something is soon recognized as wrong. But nobody can put their finger on it.

The attempt to replicate a predecessor nearly always fails. Not only is there a certain uniqueness about the human personality, but, as the poet reminds us, 'no man is an island'. If, over a period of time, a successful appointment denotes a successful team and one person leaves, a new synthesis will be required. We will need to look at the team itself; for when one leading person leaves a team, the team roles of the remaining members often become subsequently more conspicuous as they strive to bring into play not only their primary team roles but their secondary (and perhaps underfulfilled) team roles, too.

Seeking a new helmsman

The second approach commonly encountered in dealing with issues of succession emphasizes discontinuity in preference to continuity.

While the former may seem the more difficult path to tread, the likelihood of some measure of success is greater than where continuity is the goal. The reason is that discontinuity starts with a recognition that there is a problem. The problem can then be diagnosed in terms of the shortcomings of the previous incumbent for the job in question, or perhaps more significantly by a recognition that a new scenario beckons. But whatever the reason the actions are not simply reactive but are driven by a conscious analytical quest. The crucial matter is whether that quest leads somewhere. If it does, a further question is whether the analysis results in a meaningful team-role specification.

A few people can manage to end up with something similar intuitively. But if that is not feasible, a formal procedure can be followed. Under the system Interplace that we developed, a list of possible candidates with the appropriate team-role profiles could be summoned by computer search in a matter of seconds. The next step was to work through the list, striking off non-runners, in order to find the candidate who could be most confidently recommended. Here the issues that came to the fore were as follows:

1 Does the candidate seem credible, or, if not, could the candidate be made more credible by dint of some appropriate planned experience or training?
2 Is the candidate a good example of the type? Here computer analysis of the assessment data would rapidly furnish the answer.
3 Is the candidate's orientation right for taking on a particular set of responsibilities? An answer to this question could require the services of a skilled interviewer.

Needless to say, this approach is not usually followed. What happens instead is that a person's potential contribution is judged indirectly by track record and experience from which the team role is either ignored or at best presumed. For example, anyone engaged for some time in research and development or involved in a new ventures project may be taken as generally innovative, i.e. a good example of a Plant. Frequently, this turns out to be a wrong assumption. The innovative element may have been supplied by a colleague. Nevertheless, the experience gained will allow the applicant to talk about innovation in an informed, apparently enterprising and therefore convincing fashion. So the wrong conclusion is drawn.

So far we have looked at the typical problems that arise, when team roles are disregarded, or too lightly considered, when seeking a successor with particular qualifications. The mistake, some might

argue, is to place too high an emphasis on any given set of characteristics in relation to specified needs. Some prefer to look instead for
calibre. Once a person of high potential is recognized, attention can
switch to career planning. The right candidate with the right experience
will then be ready when the right moment arrives. That at least is
the theory.

The Crown Prince is waiting

An organization that takes career planning seriously has to face the
fact that short-term benefits are being sacrificed in order to secure the
looked-for long-term advantage. Proof of performance in a posting is
not a prerequisite for being moved on. Once a prince is crowned,
in the eyes of top management, the chosen individual will progress
through a series of short-stay appointments in order to widen experience
and to become acquainted with the people who matter at all stages of
the organization. It has been observed that, once this policy is followed,
the Crown Prince is bound to become King. No other candidate has
been so well prepared. The prophecy is self-fulfilling.

The Crown Prince approach has been tried by many firms but I
have yet to hear of one that is fully satisfied with the results achieved.
Even if someone of obvious calibre is found, something seems to go
wrong, often before the crown is solemnly placed on the head.

The limitation inherent in the Crown Prince strategy is that anyone
destined for stardom no longer has to struggle. Since the crucial
decision on selection has already been taken, there is little need to
sharpen personal skills and to adopt different team roles in moving
from one temporary position to another. Complacency is apt to set
in. Contrast this with what happens when several people are vying
for promotion and are being tried out in different positions. At one
moment one figure is favoured, then another. But as time goes on,
a particular candidate emerges who surpasses the others in coping
well with a greater range of problems and in handling more complex
and demanding situations. That figure with a proven performance
record is the one who will be appointed.

The term 'Crown Prince' in its application to industry has seemingly borrowed the principle that governs royal succession. There is,
however, an important distinction to be observed. Royal succession is
hereditary. In a constitutional monarchy there are no competitors,
even within a royal family, for succession is nearly always based on

primogeniture. The rigidity of the system, however, has its compensations: the heir can be prepared for the role ahead over an exceptionally long time span and there will be no disappointed contenders.

That realization raises the interesting issue as to whether it is better in succession planning to have long preparation and no selection or minimal preparation and competitive selection. The weakness of the first method is that if the candidate is not up to the mark there is no way out. Some dynasties have collapsed for that very reason. If the last Tsar of Russia had had the personal qualities of Peter the Great, perhaps the Russian Revolution would never have taken place or, if it had, it would have been unlikely to have succeeded.

The elimination of all selection possibilities carries enormous risks. In the case of the British Monarchy it was perhaps fortunate that Edward the Eighth decided to marry a divorcee, so opening the way for an objection by the Archbishop of Canterbury and the crowning of the 'runner up', George the Sixth, for had he not done so the merits of the Monarchy would almost certainly have been called into question.

Some ways of modifying Divine Right in succession

The most successful dynasties have usually provided some element of selection in succession. That is how a dynasty can be differentiated from a dictatorship and that is why dynasties survive. There are some useful lessons here that are seldom appreciated and are worth bearing in mind in the modern world.

Take some of the great dynasties of the past. A method of selection was a virtual necessity when a ruler had a number of wives. Children might be born virtually simultaneously from different mothers and some form of discrimination between them was needed to secure their relative succession rights.

Whenever an outstanding royal leader appeared, there was usually a good bet that his appearance was not merely a matter of chance. Take the case of Alexander the Great whose achievements in conquest and government over a short period must rank among the most outstanding in history. Contrary to common presumptions, he was not the oldest son of Philip of Macedon but had proved himself over other contenders by distinguished service with the army from a very early age. Such experience was important because for three centuries there had been a convention in Macedonia that governed succession.

Ratification of the nominated king could only come about when the soldiers from leading families clashed their shields together to indicate their approval. Once elected in this way the King exercised command for the rest of his life. Naturally, the soldiers would not elect someone who they knew to be a dud. The Kings of Poland were also 'elected' by a similar type of popular acclamation, although of course that privilege to acclaim belonged to a restricted circle.

Other methods of handling the succession process among rulers were cruder in nature. In the case of the long-running Ottoman Empire, the procedure introduced by Mohammed II, was to allow the Sultans to murder their brothers. This act of macabre statesmanship provided one major advantage. It ensured that succession went to the most vigorous of the contenders, while the elimination of royal rivals meant that the empire could continue undisturbed during the life of the ruler. Two centuries later the principle was modified when Achmet I, a softie by contemporary standards, ordained that fratricide should be replaced by the cageing of male heirs, thereby removing them from common sight. The Prisoner of Zenda in literature later records this tradition in another setting.

Another favoured variant among the methods of competitive royal selection has been the poisoning of rivals. So widespread was this practice that it led to food tasting becoming one of the major mediaeval service professions at court. At least the ultimate inheritor needed strong wits, and perhaps some technological interest and skill, in order to survive and reach the last round, as it were.

Given that type of competitive background it is barely conceivable that Nicholas II, the last of the Tsars, would have won through to inherit the crown of Russia. But we are now in a different era where succession practices had changed. Christianity had been adopted by the Tsars centuries earlier. Polygamy and 'the sport of kings' had been abandoned. There was a time when rulers could count their progeny in tens or even hundreds. But the change in marriage habits, by resulting in a smaller batch of offspring, limited choice in succession and virtually put an end to uncertainty in succession. If an heir proved unworthy of the throne, there was not much that could be done about it

These problems of royal succession are less remote from contemporary life than may seem at first sight, for a related dilemma occurs in the case of family businesses. The expectation is that businesses will pass from father to son. In Victorian times the successor to run the family business might be chosen from a dozen children. In the case of the modern nuclear family the choice of a successor will be limited or non-existent. Here the agenda for the next of kin shifts from one of succession, based on absolute power, to that of deciding how a member of the family should best be integrated within the firm. It has become a matter not of who but of how.

Team roles and succession

Our brief survey of methods for handling succession brings out the advantages of developing a balanced strategy. On the one hand there is a need for an elite, for it is only on the basis of an elite, howsoever chosen, that a case can be made out for developing a system of long-term career planning and preparation, where long-term advantage is bought at the expense of short-term loss. On the other hand if elitism is narrowed to the extent of meaning automatic succession of the most eligible candidate, the benefits of career planning and preparation are virtually counter-balanced by one unfortunate factor: if the chosen individual disappoints, for any reason, there is not much that can be done about it.

A proper balance can, however, be achieved where a number of possible candidates have been prepared and one of that number is to be selected. While murder has been the much practised method throughout history of arriving at a successor, the method looks open to improvement. Candidates in a stable and well-ordered society no longer have a licence to eliminate one another. That means that the privilege of recognizing and crowning a legitimate successor must pass to someone outside the contest.

During the Middle Ages that privilege belonged to the Pope whose blessing was essential for the royal Heads of State over much of Europe. The key principle was one of establishing eligibility. Only the Pope had the moral authority to decide who was the most eligible successor and to ratify that choice by placing the crown upon the head.

At this point, we need to resume where we left off in Chapter 4, when we examined the shortcomings to which appointments based on eligibility are subject and, conversely, the advantages of basing judgements on suitability. But just as someone outside the contest needs to decide who is eligible, so also someone outside the contest needs to decide who is suitable.

What we had established in Chapter 4 as a fair working hypothesis was that candidates judged suitable were predominantly good examples of their team-role type, that they had good back-up team roles, while they had also learned to manage themselves and others in team-role areas in which they were personally deficient. This skill did not mean that the most successful top managers belonged to any one given type. Different types receive their curtain call at different times as the drama of a firm's development unfolds. But the person who has an understanding of what team role to play and when to play it, and equally when it would be inadvisable to play a preferred natural role, will enjoy a lead start over others as a candidate for succession at the most senior level. This rare capacity is what is often referred to as a political skill. That term fails to do justice to the real skill content, for that term suggests an ability to manipulate others. While that element may be important, its essential foundation springs from good self-insight and good self-management.

The question that now arises is how these features are best detected in candidates who are being exposed and developed in different situations. The technology we had developed in Interplace provided an almost instant database on the team-role behaviour of candidates in different assignments and positions. There was little difficulty in interpreting what it all meant provided moves were made infrequently. Then a consistent picture would usually emerge. On the other hand, if no coherent team role stood out from the data it was normally a sign that all was not well and that no team role had been successfully established.

It was another matter when candidates were moved on at relatively frequent intervals from one position to another in order to gain experience. The fact that the assessment data registered no clear and coherent pattern could be explained in several possible ways: that colleagues had had no time to arrive at any conclusion about the newcomer; that the newcomer was acting as a supernumerary with little opportunity to display anything at all; or, finally, that the newcomer had failed to read the situation and seize the opportunity present, and so had floundered about, looking conspicuously roleless.

At first we could devise no satisfactory way of unravelling this predicament in interpretation, although closer examination of the more favourable and less favourable assessment words used by observers gave us clues. In the end we reached the conclusion that ill-considered career planning is prone to sow confusion in all directions. Established people in the work situation say: 'Why has this person been thrust upon us?' The individual in question says: 'I don't feel there is a real job here to be done.' And when that happens, the newcomer becomes an outsider who can be ganged up against.

The answer is that no-one should be brought into a work situation solely for the purpose of gaining experience. For everyone, there should be a role in view. It will not matter overmuch if that role is a functional or a team role. A person can be tried out in a number of contexts in the expectation that there will be an opportunity to make a particular contribution. Occasionally, that expectation is confounded when a person who is supposed to make one type of contribution makes another instead.

The information gained from a surprise of this nature can be a valuable pointer to a preferred team role. Surprises on functional roles are rare. But when it comes to team roles surprises are much more common. In practice, the image of most people is unduly influenced by the conventional picture surrounding their job title and experience. For example, accountants are commonly stereotyped as being individuals preoccupied with the nitty gritty and very conscientious in getting things precisely right. Occasionally, an accountant is found to display typical Resource Investigator attributes and it would be sheer agony for such a person to remain long on, say, an auditing operation. Once that team-role profile has emerged, immediate implications follow on how career development should proceed.

There is then a case for using team-role data as the primary source of information for recommending a career route. When the demands of the job, or the interpersonal chemistry involved in close group working, ideally require a particular team-role shape and that shape is available, the person will respond by giving a lot to the situation. Exactly how much, lends itself to measurement through assessment. Personal growth in this way can be examined in a variety of assignments.

On the other hand, when a person with a known team role is placed in a situation for which that team role is inappropriate, experience suggests that very little that is positive emerges from the placement. The challenge produces not personal growth but a negative reaction. One typical symptom is that several people end up blaming one another for whatever it is that has happened or for, that matter, not happened.

There are occasions when a person of considerable maturity is placed in exactly that situation and yet will succeed in rising above it. So what is the explanation?

The answer does not seem to be by being adaptable and slotting into the team role that is required, other than as a temporary measure. Instead, the seemingly ill-placed incumbent reacts by changing the situation, manages by some means to redraw a personal job boundary and negotiates with others so that in effect they redraw theirs. By the time the incumbent leaves the job it is no longer the same as it was when first entered.

Not many people behave like this but it does seem to be the mark of those who somehow succeed in making their way forward in every assignment and who eventually arrive in a top position. Nevertheless, to attempt to develop successors by giving them challenging but ill-fitting assignments is a risky business. It is an approach that can either bring out the best in people or go badly wrong.

A strategy for fail-safe succession

To groom a single individual for the top position over a prolonged period is not a strategy that can be recommended. Not only is it possible that the wrong choice has been made and someone promising in one situation turns out to be disappointing in another, but when the moment of succession arrives, another type of person is required. 'Cometh the hour, cometh the man', as the saying goes.

The only advisable strategy in preparing for succession is to groom a small stock of elite candidates of varying dispositions and attributes in the hope that any one of them would make a reasonable final choice.

A good spread of team roles is an essential requirement here, since over a period of time a firm may find itself in a number of different situations. An enterprise that needs to make tough decisions to improve its financial viability is best headed by a Shaper, one that needs to change its position in the market place may be better served by a Plant, while one that needs to consolidate could best be run by an Implementer. All three, however, would need candidates who were good examples of the type. However, even a good example of the type is liable to prove a disappointment if given an unsuitable position of responsibility. For example, an enterprise that has survived a period of turmoil and now needs an interval of peaceful consolidation is not going to be well served by a strong Shaper or a visionary Plant.

There are exceptions to this rule where the appointee has enough self-insight and team-role knowledge to recognize the predicament. In that case the appointee may surprise working associates by behaving in a way that conflicts with the expectations attached to the position. I have known a number of individuals who were considered by associates in that situation to have acted 'strangely' (i.e. by not following textbook behaviour) but to have 'got away with it'. This strangeness is in effect a form of sophistication. Yet the need to depart from expectation is a sure sign that the appointee is not a 'natural' for the position and has developed other means of dealing with the situation.

It is our contention that the best appointments are naturals. A high-calibre candidate who is not a natural may perform satisfactorily but inwardly will recognize an aptitude for another type of appointment and will probably not stay.

In claiming that successors should be naturals, we are not reducing the magnitude of the problem, but, rather, we are projecting an ideal. Unlike royal succession, we have a great number of people on whom we can draw. But the advantage is only there provided we can screen the field effectively. It means that the potential of a promising person should have been recognized at an earlier stage, then 'proved' in competition with others in a variety of testing assignments; and finally that suitability is established on the basis of the right calibre and team role for the part in the context of the organization's scenario once the moment of succession has arrived.

That recipe sounds a mouthful, which perhaps is right, for it is a tall order. If only part of this formula is followed, at least the chances increase that some prospective disaster on the part of those who lead us will have been averted.

12 *The future shape of organization*

This book has taken the theme that if people are to make an effective contribution at work, they need a role that equips them to work with others. In the pre-industrial past, such a role scarcely needed thinking about for it was governed by factors that were largely physical such as gender, age or race, and so was beyond the control of the individual. At a later stage the immediate visible factors that signified the role became less conspicuous. But there were cues that could be acquired and displayed, such as certificates that entitled or privileged a person to practise a trade, often reinforced by distinctive clothing that would confirm the role in the eyes of the onlooker.

As history has given way to modern times, what may be perceived as a pre-emptive claim on a role has largely disappeared. People do not know what their role is or should be. Valued roles have become difficult to acquire because there is no regular preparation for them. Yet those who fail to establish a role are in some jeopardy for, should that failure continue, the prospects are bleak. Bleakest of all are the prospects of those who have never entered the labour force or those who have held jobs for only limited periods of time. For these, the ultimate danger of rolelessness is that they drift into the Underclass, so adding to what may well become the biggest problem of the twenty-first century.

So it is in the interests of society as a whole that each fit and able adult member becomes, or should have been, both a contributor and a beneficiary; a contributor as a provider of goods, services or money, as well as a beneficiary of the wealth that economic synergy produces. Equally, it is in the interests of employers that the complementary role strengths of those it employs should be used in the most effective way to serve its principal goals and objectives, just as it is in the interest of the individual to play a role that is both self-fulfilling and appreciated by others.

This type of enrolment and mutuality, operating both at the level of the employing firm and society as a whole, may appear an abstraction.

Yet I will argue in this chapter that the problems to which they give rise and the solutions available are related. What binds them together on the positive side is something that involves a type of leadership and organization.

A century in turmoil

Before I attempt to spell out a theme about the relationship between the individual, the team and the organization, it may be instructive for the moment to take a broad historical view and glance back at the century that is closing. While this has been marked by the greatest explosion in history in terms of population growth and material output, its negative features are equally notable. Vast numbers have paid with their lives in conflicts that in human terms have brought no winners.

The prime movers in the events that have disfigured the century have been individuals elevated into supreme positions of power as Dictators, Generalissimos and 'Presidents for Life'. In restrospect, we are bound to ask: What made them successful in the first place? What have we to learn from their rise that can reduce the chances that the same thing may happen again? What needs to be done to modify the models of leadership and organization they created and which evidently won such wide appeal?

At the personal level, it is plain that the ascendency of the twentieth century dictators is attributable to certain qualities of leadership that, even if perverted, are commonly valued: to some vision of the future; to an ability to project that vision; and to inspire in others commitment to a greater Cause.

But the establishment of tyranny and the successful exploitation of human gullibility demands additional talents. Here one can single out in particular a flair for persuading the masses that corporate identity should replace personal identities. Individual views are then sacrificed for the togetherness of the totalitarian or fundamentalist state. In effect, the loss of individuality opens the way to the binding interpretation, ruling and judgement of the charismatic Leader on all major issues. By denying the scope for individual role playing, the way is prepared for total followership.

The political Solo Leader, however, cannot travel far on the basis of charisma alone. Substantial organizational structures and systems have been needed to turn the ambitions of the Solo Leader into accomplishment.

The first step in this process has been the building up of a tightly disciplined and personally controlled Party; the second, the formation of an elaborate multi-tiered command structure within the state itself; and the third and final stage has been the creation of an elaborate bureaucracy designed to supervise minutely everything that was being controlled. The cost of eliminating internal challenge in this way has been the stifling of all initiative.

Now, with reference to the subject matter of this book, the vocabulary of the team and of team roles could never find a place within such a framework. Teams need a degree of autonomy for their operation. They generate a momentum of their own that is capable of challenging Authority: that is why they are anathema to dictators. Further, since teams are inclined to form spontaneously, as in informal groups, free association had to be curbed. To this end all manner of mechanisms have been devised to prevent autonomous groups from forming.

In spite of the temporary success of the totalitarian systems of the twentieth century, the facts of the matter show they were short-lived by historical standards. Some lasted no more than a few years. And even those that lasted for some decades degenerated rapidly in vigour. In the case of the USSR and its satellites, a whole collection of states finally imploded without any external pressure. In spite of an almost unprecedented concentration of power, no dynasties were established that looked set to rival the long-lasting Ottoman or Mogul Empires in earlier centuries.

The twentieth century was put to enormous trouble in containing the Rogue States. In the eyes of some, they were considered efficient in their early days. But they were not efficient enough to survive. In that sense, they proved more fragile than the tyrannies in earlier eras. They fell because they contained organizational flaws which the twentieth century was able to expose.

Dynamic tyrants in the Corporation

It may be useful at this point to turn our attention to the nature of Corporations and large manufacturing firms, for the history of these organizations bears comparison with that of their political counterparts during the same era.

Mass production had its legendary beginnings with the manufacture of the first popular motor car. Henry Ford I not only produced cars but he gave his name to Fordism. All work was broken down into small standard elements that could be performed repetitiously by workers. There was no allowance for individuality or teamwork, or even for rest periods. It was a system brilliantly portrayed on film by Charlie Chaplin in *Modern Times*. This era figured the bigshot. The word of the boss was law. Opposition was not sanctioned. Union organizers, or so-called troublemakers, were 'taken for a ride'. The phrase that has stayed in the English language referred originally to the operations of Pinkertons. These were members of a hired agency who would identify individuals that were considered to be opponents or potential opponents, bundle them into a car, beat them up and dump them in a ditch.

It was not only the Model T car that spread but the political and employer practices that went with it. These features migrated from North America, where they died out, to South America where they enjoyed a much longer run. Bigshots had their fingers in both the industrial and political pies. They ran the system from above, made great sums of money for themselves and brooked no opposition. The bloated capitalist epitomized the system. The ill practices of that system and the philosophy that went with it were underscored by the spread of Marxism. At a popular level they were expressed through satire. What Charlie Chaplin conveyed in the cinema, Bertolt Brecht communicated on the stage. The capitalist tycoon was characterized as both a business and political racketeer.

What this imagery obscured from public perception is that capitalism in its classic form is a morally neutral economic system for generating and using the finance needed for investment. Capitalism may be contrasted with egalitarianism but it is nevertheless social in nature, for the spread of risk involves many people. It is out of character that such a system should depend on all-powerful individuals. It is in keeping that in the democratic industrial world, at least, tycoons who have overreached themselves have been dethroned by the system they reputedly epitomized. There is a long catalogue of those who, unable to fix things with the powers that be, have landed up in prison charged with financial malpractice and deception of one sort or another. Those who were able to run their empires as Solo Leaders acting as though answerable only to themselves have regularly failed to transfer that style to political leadership unless, as has happened in a number of cases, through the seizure of total power.

In the long run, capitalism can never sanction a self-oriented style of management or one where self-interest is allowed to operate at the expense of collective interest. When other people's money is being used, some form of control is bound to be exercised and a proper system of accountability introduced. As capitalism acquired an increasingly social character (with the prime players often being the managers of pension funds) and as it grew to embrace ever-widening spheres of social and political influence, the scope for the unbridled tycoon diminished.

Industrial empires in decline

The growth of industrial Corporations in the early part of the century depended much on single individuals with big personal reputations. The hero entrepreneur not only saw opportunities but attracted investors. Nevertheless, belief in the hero entrepreneur needed to be sustained. The creation of confidence demanded a track record of continuous growth and expansion.

Many Corporations in tune with this need developed an overly aggressive appetite for gobbling up smaller firms. The take-over bid became the order of the day. Such ambition has been justified by some on the grounds that benefits arise from economies of scale. Yet bigness is difficult to reconcile with personal control. As the century progressed, big was no longer regarded as beautiful, even in the world of business. Expansion may be needed to build up confidence in the leader of an enterprise, but appetitive expansion has often been the harbinger of disappointing company results. The lesson from retrospective analysis of so many take-over bids is a poor return on the capital invested.

That lesson took a long time to learn. This is because financial figures can be disguised in the short term: accounts can be consolidated or temporary success highlighted by resorting to loose auditing practices or the deliberate hiding of essential information. But when the ultimate truth has emerged and the position of the expansionist industrial Moguls has proved untenable before meetings of their Boards or their shareholders, they have been fired or pensioned-off. And as the mighty have fallen, Corporations have set about reversing the process. Acquisitions have been halted and peripheral businesses have been hived off in order to improve liquidity.

This common pattern of events, which has been much in evidence in the second half of the century, can be explained in something other than economic terms: human factors often set the limits to growth. The single individual, in order to justify himself to his backers, has been tempted to venture beyond his capacity for personal control. The process has then moved into reverse gear and the emphasis has shifted back from the individual to the group. So, as industrial empires have collapsed, or have been forced to contract under pressure, management buyouts have been to the fore in purchasing the parts of the empire. And it is a common experience that loss-making enterprises have then become profitable. That lesson has not been lost on investors. Management buyouts are now viewed with favour by merchant banks and the necessary funds are soon forthcoming.

So what general conclusion can be reached about the rise and fall of industrial empires?

Even if there are risks in reaching any generalization, there is a good deal of support for the view that, as the century has progressed, the cult of the Solo Leader has receded, while the reputation of the autonomous management team has been enhanced.

If that view is upheld by continued evidence, part of the reason must lie with the fact that managers have improved their knowledge and understanding of how to operate as a team. They have learned how best to reconcile personal growth with mutual support.

A general crisis at the centre of hierarchy

To sum up so far, we have noted some parallels between the operations of Solo Leaders, whether in the aggressive mega-state or in expansionist mega-corporations; in the multi-tiered control structures to which they give rise; and in the decay in their efficiency.

In an earlier chapter we examined the way in which this decay was intrinsic to Solo Leadership. There are benefits in having a single talented leader, who can grasp the total picture; but these benefits are liable to be dissipated in large complex organizations as crucial mistakes are made which cannot be communicated to the Solo Leader (or the messenger will be shot) nor admitted without damage to the Leader's public image.

There is, however, one weakness that afflicts hierarchy and operates independently of the character of the person at the top. Nor is it primarily a matter of personal talent. The problem lies in the nature of the organization itself; for particular types of organization go with particular types of leader. Solo Leaders need a system designed to transmit the leader's message with clarity and purity to every level of the organization. Such systems are designed for downward communication. Formal in nature, they are ideal for transmitting messages that expect compliance.

The weakness of conventional hierarchies was demonstrated classically in the First World War when Field Marshall Haig conceived an offensive across the Somme. As it happened the chosen battleground was a quagmire. Of course, in the eyes of those at the front the plan was not feasible. But the message in its purest form never penetrated the intermediary layers of officers to reach the man at the top. The price of this strategic bloomer was one hundred thousand lives: the gain a few yards of muddy territory.

Many multi-tiered organizations are constructed to be run along the lines of Field Marshall Haig's army. Such organizations may be likened to a motor coach where the driver sits not at the wheel but at the rear of the vehicle. At each bend those in the front row pass on the message about the lie of the road to those in the row behind. They in turn pass back the message until it reaches the man at the back who provides the commands. It will not be long before the coach is in the ditch.

In flexible organizations communication is a two-way business, with upward communication the more difficult leg in the cycle.

Where information does move upwards it tends to do so along informal channels. Technically, that information is not easy to receive, even with the best will in the world and few hierarchical organizations have established mechanisms for receiving it anyway. So the old downward-driven hierarchies tend to persist. They will go on persisting until they are reformed. Whatever may be involved in reform should encompass changed relationships between the individual, the team and the organization.

The nature of these changes that might be foreshadowed for the twenty-first century need to be considered for both the public and private sectors.

Organization in the public sector

The most regimented and multi-layered organizations in the modern world are to be found in the Departmental functions of Government in large countries. These Departments and Ministries are there to transmit downwards and administer standard policies conceived on high, irrespective of their applicability at local level. Once those policies are drawn up, even the most senior officials have to observe the rules. Since most procedures, systems and entitlements are backed up by law or enactment, they are not easily circumvented or modified. There is little for the exercise of common sense on the part of intelligent executives.

The rigidity in the mode of management that results is well illustrated by a personal experience when talking to the UK Civil Service College. It has long been my declared position that if managers are to be held accountable for the effectiveness of their operations they should choose their own team: 'We can't do that in the Civil Service', I have been regularly told. 'We have to take the people we are given'. However persuasive the argument it would seem to have very little bearing on what actually happens. That is determined by the structure and tradition of the system rather than by any set of individual, or even collective, decisions.

It has been argued by some that the rigidity of the Civil Service is due to the mentality of those who are attracted into it. I have to say that I do not accept that explanation of the problem. As it happens, I have collected a large body of material on the team roles of UK Civil Servants and have access to some comparable material for Australian Civil Servants. In both cases there is a wide spread of available team roles and indeed there is a very adequate supply of officials whose profiles are quite entrepreneurial. There has to be another explanation for the inertness of bureaucracy. That explanation, I believe, lies in the number of tiers that characterize the hierarchy of officialdom. The problem, in other words, is akin to the Field Marshall Haig phenomenon.

Consider the case alluded to earlier, of the challenge posed to society by large numbers of roleless, jobless people. These are denied a role in a team and, in a state of desperation and demoralization, are in danger of being drawn into the Underclass. This problem, in the eyes of the public, is considered to belong to the public sector. Both politicians and public servants are therefore expected to make an attack on it. The offensive is planned at the top. The tactics and instructions are passed down to junior ranks. Eventually, the social offensive, like the military offensive, peters out at great cost to the tax-paying public. What has gone wrong?

I have drawn on my experiences* in working on international projects relating to the unemployed to draw up a different scenario for tackling these problems. The efficient use of resources, the development of professionalism and the need to treat people in a personal way cannot be managed without discretion at the local level and the

---

* See Belbin, M., *The Job Promoters: A Journey to a New Profession*, Butterworth-Heinemann, Oxford, 1990.

devolving of power. But hardly anywhere is this happening. For mega politics is about power and its centralization, which takes us through the controlling mechanisms of hierarchy to the Solo Leader.

Simple organizations are the most dynamic

A system that produces efficient downward communication is easy to construct. A system that covers efficient upward communication is far more difficult to contrive. But of one thing we can be certain, levels are very prone to become barriers in upward communication.

A law that we may put forward is that inefficiency in hierarchical bureaucracies is broadly commensurate with the number of command levels in an organization. With flatter organizations, communication shifts from down and up to mainly lateral relationships.

In so shifting, delayering offers the prospect of increased efficiency. But this benefit will only materialize if the organization tackles a number of social issues.

With fewer chains in command there needs to be more teamwork. Getting on with colleagues calls for personal qualities that differ from a capacity for finding favour with the boss. There is, too, the problem that difficult but talented individuals may not operate well in a team. It will demand new learning from them just as the team itself needs to acquire experience on how such individuals are best assimilated.

Another pressing problem relates to career expectations. We live in a world in which the notion of promotion is uppermost in the minds of the most able and aspiring within an organization. At one time a regular response to these pressures was to create posts with higher-sounding titles. There were assistant managers, deputy directors, liaison officers, and others, who had no troops to command but who at the same time did not belong in the ranks. All would seek to carve out roles for themselves. These intermediaries have increased the complexity of organization enormously.

As hierarchies become delayered and as more autonomous groups become empowered to find and manage their own resources in pursuit of their objectives, career expectations will need to point in some new direction. Personal growth will be accomplished through broadening of experience rather than through elevation in status. Those who belong to a team will develop by widening their functional and technical skills while still retaining their individual team-role identity. There will be interchange of members between teams. There will be a need to play an effective part in a wide number of settings and with a different mix of people, all of which will demand new skills in self-management. Those who acquire and display these arts will be the people who will succeed. By nature, they will have little in common with the Solo Leaders who so disfigured a century of turmoil.

Three forms of coming organization — the shamrock, the honeycomb and the trapezium

Organizations have been evolving, as we have seen, over the last century; so that the future is already written into parts of the present and has thereby lent itself to observation. Nevertheless, the evolving pattern is not always recognized.

Here, a useful view has been put forward by Charles Handy in *The Age of Unreason.* He has drawn attention to what he calls the Shamrock pattern of organization. The shamrock, the Irish national emblem, is a small plant. It has a clover-like leaf that consists of three leaflets attached to a common stalk. The parts are separate and yet they belong to the whole. So, too, the organization of the developing present and of the future. One leaflet embodies the core professional workers, a second the variable part-time labour force and the third the contractors who belong outside the firm itself and yet who make an essential contribution to the business.

What this pattern tells us, in other words, is that the gigantism of earlier organizations is breaking down. It reinforces the view that the world is moving towards smaller teams. We see it in terms of leaflets rather than large compound leaves.

Sub-contracting offers flexibility in operations. That is why an increasing number of firms are seeing advantages in persuading skilled but expensive employees to offer their services in autonomous units operating from the outside. They become a charge rather than an overhead. But the link is still important. The principal company acts like a foster parent, nurturing even to the extent of providing some of the capital to encourage the separation. It is like a down payment on a flat provided by a parent to assist a young adult to move into a separate establishment.

The increasing number of units that appear autonomous yet are in fact linked suggests a honeycomb. These cells are packed in close proximity but the bees still need a queen bee to keep them together. The queen is not a Solo Leader but has an important, though limited,

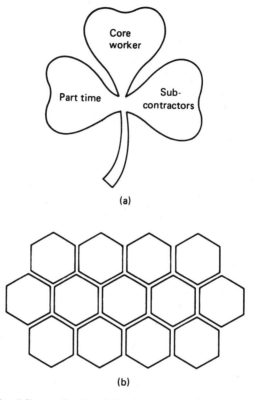

(a)

(b)

Small firms gather in cellular clusters as in a honeycomb

Figure 12.1 *Visions of organization: (a) The shamrock organization (after Handy, C. (1989),* The Age of Unreason, *Hutchinson); (b) The honeycomb organization (after Porter, M. (1990),* The Competitive Edge of Nations, *Macmillan)*

part to play which is as distinctive as that of the other bees. It is the combined division of labour and the functional interdependence that enables bees to make a success of the hive.

The implication of what is argued is that some units will thrive best as autonomous work groups, linked with others through an attachment of interest and working in close proximity. They may, for example, share certain facilities, which means in effect that they use them more economically than would otherwise be the case. These units are the right size for what they do. They have all sorts of other advantages in co-existing in proximity, as Michael Porter has reminded us in his well researched *The Competitive Edge of Nations* (Macmillan 1990). And the fact that they are grouped enables them to present an enhanced public relations image to the outside world and protects them from the trading limitations and uncertainties that attach to smallness. Let us suppose that all the small firms in so-called Silicon Valley in the USA or all the small financial offices in the City of London were scattered throughout the land. Would they be able to carry on as usual? Clearly not. They owe their existence to the fact that they are packed together in a hive. They are part of a honeycomb.

While small firms thrive under certain conditions, bigness in other circumstances does confer certain advantages, especially economies of scale. The fundamental problem is not whether bigness is bad in itself but whether bigness can be detached from bureaucracy.

It is this realization that prompts the concept of the Trapezium organization. Here a few words need to be said by way of introduction.

We have postulated earlier that bureaucracy is related less to bigness than to the number of tiers within an organization. That distinction has not been sufficiently addressed in the past, primarily for the reason that bigness and the multi-tiered organization were co-terminous.

Large organizations spawn a multiplicity of levels for two reasons:

1 The first reason is connected with the pressure for personal advancement and the personal expectations of employees within every successful organization. The reaction to this pressure is for management to offer promotion through a system of career progression through salary grading. The by-product of this system is an extension of the status hierarchy and increasing complications in the social systems.

2 The second force operating is the assumed need to exercise closeness of control. In practice, this usually takes the form of eyeball-to-eyeball supervision, which in turn affects the way in which the firm is structured.

Once it becomes accepted that intimate personal relations are needed between the managers and the managed, then certain things follow: the span of control; the number of levels; and the size of the workforce become interrelated mathematically.

A very different situation prevails when power is transferred to autonomous work groups, for which a prerequisite is the dismantling of formal hierarchy. Even so, people still have to be managed, resources allocated, personnel switched and career progressions arranged.

This is where the distinction needs to be made between strategic management and operational management. Both have a complementary part to play in maintaining the vitality of the enterprise. The two should never be confused and the case for strategic management is commonly neglected. Switching resources from one type of activity to another provides a means of ensuring that new promising enterprises are entered into and that obsolete ones are dropped.

There is, therefore, a case for advocating two levels of organization, one strategic and the other operational. What we will argue here is that no other levels are needed. Indeed, intermediary levels merely serve to clog up the system.

The corollary of this hypothesis is that the organization should be very flat. If there are only two levels of management, eyeball-to-eyeball supervision is scarcely feasible. For most of the time, people need to be self-managing as individuals or self-managing in a team. In so far as they are managed from above, as they still will be to some extent, the controlling factor will be through data. Information technology will indicate how well the team or the individual is doing. While there will be room for discussion, the basic fact remains that when responsibility is delegated, those who perform inadequately should be replaced and moved into more suitable positions rather than pressurized into a major conversion in behaviour.

Changing the team to advantage is relatively easy for strategic managers once good data are available. That is because progress with information technology has brought about an entirely new situation. Users at the most senior level can now know more about the attributes of individuals and their suitability for the jobs they hold than a single on-the-spot supervisor. The span of effective control begins to stretch towards infinity.

Of course, there are practical constraints. These arise not because the data cannot be handled and their meanings acted on, but because people need people if morale is to be maintained. Strategic managers need to talk to operational managers in order to be kept in touch, even if there are no pressing issues on the agenda. Walk-about-management may not appeal to strategic managers but some of it is almost certainly necessary if they are not to become remote in their understanding of what is really going on.

Given these two recommended levels of management, it becomes plain that no recommended span of personal control looks justified. All we can say is that an organization should comprise only a small team of strategic managers and that these should be capable of servicing a large number of semi-autonomous units run by teams of operational managers. In effect, the old multi-tiered pyramid is broken down to resemble a trapezium.

A trapezium has two parallel sides. Strategic management and operational management are both operating in a flat plane, since they embody teamwork, but the higher plane is notably smaller than the lower plane. The two other sides of this four-sided figure can be at almost any acute angle since the span of control is not fixed but is variable. The whole model is designed to allow team management to function effectively. Solo Leaders would find it very difficult to establish a personal power base under a system of Trapezium Management.

A vision of the future

The issues examined in this chapter have been wide-ranging. That is because the containment of conflict, the management of team roles, the structure of organizations and the sort of things that organizations can and cannot accomplish are all intimately connected.

The spread of information technology will exert its influence on the structure of organizations as controls take on a new form. Supervision will depend less on the brow-beating personality and more on easily accessed and shared information. People will work to well-understood goals based on clear criteria. And as close and continuous supervision from above recedes, there will be more scope for semi-autonomous work groups. Flatter organizations will result. The decline of the typical organizational pyramid will make it progressively more difficult for a Solo Leader to seize power; more difficult to provide the conditions favouring the rise of Rogue States.

The spread of education generally is exerting an effect in the same direction. A well-educated population is less likely to accept the word of the big boss. Decisions increasingly demand consultation, a process best accomplished through peer-group relations. Hierarchy becomes less respected and compliance more difficult to enforce. In other words, social conditions are reinforcing information technology in eroding centralized power.

The acceptance of the need for small, well-composed teams will resolve many of the problems with which the twentieth century has been beset. The more effective management of team roles will serve to advance the case for small, well-balanced, working groups. Individual identities and corporate identities will no longer pull in opposite directions and will become easier to reconcile.

The Traditional Hierarchy
- with small reporting span and personal accountability

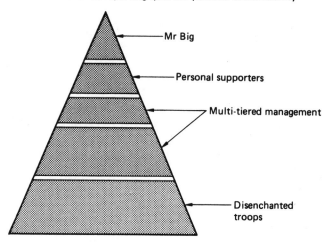

Mr Big

Personal supporters

Multi-tiered management

Disenchanted troops

Trapezium Management
- with wide reporting span and team accountability

Strategic managers
in balanced team

Mission

Power devolved
to operational
managers

Motivated
groups

Where the advantages of centralization are being obtained the Traditional
Hierarchy is being replaced by a trunkated triangle i.e. a Trapezium

Figure 12.2   *The traditional hierarchy and trapezium management*

The residual problems of the twenty-first century will focus on those who are left outside the system. These problems will be misperceived by many as economic — as primarily about income support. Others will prefer to focus on an educational shortfall in the jobless, in spite of the fact that many of the jobless will have rejected education and the values it embraces.

These pose major problems in their own right. But the more pressing matter, if the likely downward spiral is not to accelerate, will be to resist the rise of the Underclass (by which we mean those who neither engage in work or seek it but gain income in other ways) and to re-engage those who have dropped out. It will happen only if we can find them a role, a role they will accept, a role that enables them to relate to others and to contribute to work — not only a functional role but also a team role.

It will take all our energies to enrol the roleless; to create and restore personal and work identities in those on the fringes of society. That will be the coming challenge awaiting the twenty-first century.

Appendix *Establishing the team-role demands of jobs*

While skills and knowledge can be acquired by training and experience, they are insufficient by themselves to ensure suitability for a job. Stress and other problems tend to be created when the demands of a particular form of work conflict with the natural or preferred behaviour of the job-holder.

Research into the level of compatibility between the demands of work and the job-holder has resulted in the development of a Job Requirement Exercise. The inputs are computer processed to form a JRE person specification report and a compatibility report on a candidate's suitability for the job. Once the mechanism has been set up, the system will rapidly present in ranked order the most suitable candidates. Advancing technology is in this way contributing to new patterns in career development.

A brief overview of one output from the system is given below. Here a Job Requirement Answer Sheet has been completed in accordance with detailed instructions and guidelines given in a separate booklet (Figure A.1).

The example relates to a real job set up by one local government authority. The candidate considered is the one thrown up by computer search for compatibility with the job demands irrespective of eligibility. All the outputs are computer outputs, including the comments based on the personal qualities of the candidate obtained by scanning word frequencies from observer assessments. Only the name of the candidate has been changed.

JOB REQUIREMENT ANSWER SHEET

PROCEDURE: The assessor should first read fully the Job Requirement Instruction Sheet before assessing the job. Then for each of the 16 factors place one X in one of the boxes A – E. Remember that the assessment relates to the job demands and not how the person performs in the job. Finally consider the top three factors.

RATING KEY:
A – Critical
B – Important
C – Useful
D – Irrelevant
E – Unhelpful

Title of Job **SENIOR PERSONNEL OFFICER**

Name of Assessor **C.D.**   Date **7-1-93**

Section I TASK DEMANDS

	A	B	C	D	E
1. **AUTONOMY**		X			
2. **ASSIDUITY**			X		
3. **METICULOUSNESS**		X			
4. **PREPAREDNESS**		X			

Section II DEALING WITH PEOPLE

	A	B	C	D	E
5. **ASCENDENCY**		X			
6. **CO-ORDINATION**	X				
7. **DIPLOMACY**	X				
8. **MAKING CONTACTS**			X		

Section III WORK CONDITIONS AND CONSTRAINTS

	A	B	C	D	E
9. **ROBUSTNESS**		X			
10. **TOLERANCE OF ROUTINE**		X			
11. **TOLERANCE OF UNCERTAINTY**		X			
12. **SHARED RESPONSIBILITIES**		X			

Section IV DEMANDS ON MENTAL ABILITY, EXPERIENCE AND TRAINING

	A	B	C	D	E
13. **ORIGINALITY**		X			
14. **ANALYSIS**		X			
15. **EXPERIENCE AND EXPERTISE**	X				
16. **STRATEGIC OVERVIEW**		X			

OF THE SIXTEEN FACTORS ASSESSED THE THREE MOST IMPORTANT IN THIS JOB ARE (BY FACTOR NUMBER)

FIRST **6**   SECOND **7**   THIRD **15**

Figure A.1

Candidate's compatibility with the job

Job title: Senior Personnel Officer
Name of candidate: John Smith

**This job requires
(in ranked order)**: CO TW IMP RI SH   ME SP CF PL
**The candidate
has this profile**: TW CO ME SP IMP PL CF RI SH

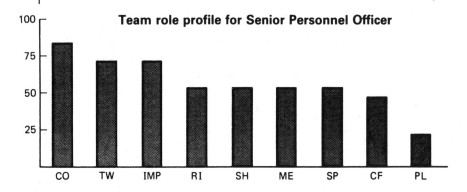

Team role profile for Senior Personnel Officer

The job as it is specified requires someone who has the capacity for drawing the best out of others, encouraging them to contribute and to identify personally with group objectives. Such a person should be able to conduct meetings in a mature fashion and in a way that allows participants to feel satisfied when proceedings have been concluded. The job also demands someone who can handle a wide range of individuals including difficult people with diplomacy and discretion. Social skills are very important to the key demands of this job. The likely candidate would be well received by others, create few enemies and be generally helpful and supportive. The job also demands someone with an organized approach to work and a capacity for dealing efficiently with matters of a practical nature. The ideal candidate will thrive in well-structured situations, be ready to assess what is feasible and show down-to-earth common sense that takes account of the needs of the organization.

The appointee should make a reliable employee, stand up well to the pressures of work and show stability in character and temperament.

The work entails a fair degree of socially proactive behaviour and a readiness to get out and about and meet people. Also needed is some level of drive and a willingness to face up to occasional opposition. Also needed is some level of planning and thinking combined with level headed judgement. Also needed is some level of technical knowledge and experience and to be a self starter within a defined field.

On this specification the ability to orchestrate a structure that is already in place is more important than the ability to open up new avenues.

John Smith is a very good fit with the job specification. He is seen as broad in outlook, calm and confident, and consultative, which is valuable for this particular position.

John Smith should be able to cope well with co-ordinating people and at steering group effort. Likely to make an effective contribution in working out priorities and formulating worth-while goals. He has the necessary listening and supportive qualities and should contribute well to the fostering of team spirit. Probably able to cope with any necessary planning and organizing that the job entails.

Figure A.2

Index